A TRIBUTE TO HOCKEY'S DEFINING MOMENTS

(Previous page) The Montreal
Canadiens, circa 1911–15, pose with
a rival team. The Canadiens, with CA
on their sweaters, haven't adopted
the legendary CH yet. Didier Pitre
kneels on the right. Georges Vezina,
in the toque, seems a bit aloof.

MICHAEL McKINLEY

ETCHED IN ICE

GREYSTONE BOOKS

Douglas & McIntyre
VANCOUVER/TORONTO

For my father, Frank, who always knows the score

Text copyright © 1998 by Michael McKinley

98 99 00 01 02   5 4 3 2 1

Greystone Books
A division of Douglas & McIntyre Ltd.
1615 Venables Street
Vancouver, British Columbia
V5L 2H1

Canadian Cataloguing in Publication Data

McKinley, Michael, 1961–
Etched in ice

ISBN 1-55054-654-6

1. Hockey—History—Anecdotes. 2. National Hockey League—Anecdotes. I. Title.
GV846.5.M24 1998   796.962   C98-910813-9

Editing by Michael Carroll
Jacket and text design by Peter Cocking
Photo research by Andrew Bergant
Front jacket photograph of Maurice Richard courtesy UPI/Corbis-Bettman
Back jacket photograph of Bobby Orr courtesy London Life—Portnoy/Hockey Hall of Fame
Printed and bound in Canada by Friesens
Printed on acid-free paper ∞

The publisher gratefully acknowledges the support of the Canada Council for the Arts
and of the British Columbia Ministry of Tourism, Small Business and Culture.
The publisher also acknowledges the financial support of the Government of Canada
through the Book Publishing Industry Development Program.

CONTENTS

INTRODUCTION

Shortly after noon on Thursday, September 28, 1972, I learned the meaning of ecstasy.

Less than a month into Grade 6, I was housebound with a nasty cold I caught from my father. So, while the nation gathered in schoolrooms, offices and bars to watch the last reel of the hockey psychodrama between virtuous Canada and the perfidious Soviets, the world's second oldest virus conspired to put me and my dad in our family room, watching history on the Electrohome colour television.

My father was cheering for the Soviets—not in malice, but as only an Irish immigrant could. Despite his gratitude to Canada for being the proverbial port in the storm, his transatlantic baggage carried that ancient Irish gift for merriment in the face of inevitable doom. Even though he wanted victory for the lads wearing the stylized maple leaf—an emblem he defended three decades earlier on the battlefields of Europe—he felt compelled to repeatedly praise the Soviets' superior strategy and discipline in face of the Canadians' anarchy.

I saw this as a paternal favour, one that allowed me to view life as a little history of calamity punctuated by infrequent and brief moments of triumph. With the series tied at three games apiece and one draw, Canada had the heavy duty of winning the eighth and last game to win back the country's national honour. It was an honour my fellow 11-year-olds and I acutely felt in peril that September as we cinched on our roller skates with our fathers' old neckties to play hockey on schoolyard asphalt—the closest

Georges Vezina, the archetypal tragic goalie, had never missed a game since his discovery by the Montreal Canadiens in 1911. Fifteen years later, after one period of shutout hockey, a feverish Vezina collapsed in goal, bleeding from the tuberculosis that would kill him on March 24, 1926, age 39. The Canadiens immortalized "the Chicoutimi Cucumber" with the Vezina Trophy for the NHL's best goalie.

we would ever come to "ice" on the streets of Vancouver. Though we happily claimed to be Phil Esposito or Ken Dryden as we skated into the waning summer (and a head cold), our gods had been shown up as mortal, and now, at the end of the second period of Canada's last chance for redemption, the team was down five goals to three.

And then the miracle began, first with Esposito's goal, then with Yvan Cournoyer's. The game was now tied, and if it stayed that way, the Soviets would win everything on aggregate goals. Then the man who had won the last two games for Canada made it a biblical thrice, smashing the puck past a mortified Vladislav Tretiak to win it all with 34 seconds left. As Paul Henderson leaped in exultation on the ice, I spun in dervish jubilation, for life would never, could never, be better than this. My surprised father cheered, too. And so there we were, two small voices in the chorus of national ecstasy.

We had all gone into the 1972 series with hockey as our birthright; we came out of it with our eyes bug-open and our hearts in our mouths. We had seen the enemy, and they were shockingly good—so good, in fact, that they would change "our game." As such, that harrowing, emotional triumph in 1972 has been chosen for this book as one of hockey's defining moments, because to leave it out would be treasonous.

The other people and events between these pages share equal majesty with that moment, for though theirs might not be as gloriously or nationalistically do-or-die, they all share an essential quality: they changed the sport or their society, and often they did both. For all, a "moment" doesn't mean a brief and isolated beat of time, but the zeniths and nadirs in the ongoing epic of the sport.

There is no moment that historians can point to as the "big bang" of hockey, but we do know that on the night of March 3, 1875, James George Alwyn Creighton, a walrus-moustached engineer who claimed all of 25 years, performed a singular act that changed the game forever.

On that night, Creighton and 17 of his Montreal friends played hockey under the filigreed, iron-beamed roof of Montreal's tony Victoria Skating Rink, watched by 40 of their curious friends and sweethearts. To us, the hockey those revolutionaries played was a primitive ancestor. There were no goal nets, but rather, metal posts marking the goal; there were no lines on the ice, and the game was played much like rugby still is, with no forward passing allowed. The players wore no padding, and their skate blades were strapped to their boots, or in some cases, screwed into the sole. Goalies, forced to stand to make a save, wore no padding, either, and were protected only by their wits.

Yet when this hour-long match was over, James Creighton had captained his team to a 2–1 victory, and an international sporting drama had begun. Until then hockey had been an expansive, free-wheeling game played only on frozen ponds and rivers in eastern Canada and New England. By putting a roof on hockey, Creighton began the process by which it would become a sport, defining it through its constraints: rules, space and the expectations of its audience. By moving hockey away from the glare of the winter sun on the outdoor ice, Creighton refocussed the light on the indoor stage, throwing into relief the people and events who would stand out against time and space in a brilliance of their own.

The Montreal Amateur Athletic Association squad of 1893 is included as a moment because it was the first to win one of professional sport's most coveted prizes, even if it refused to accept Lord Stanley's shiny new trophy. Its primacy collides with Conn Smythe's bloody-minded revenge three decades later on the New

York swells who cheated him out of a Stanley Cup, and fuelled his drive to build a Cup winner in Toronto—and a shrine for "Canada's Team." And both moments stand muted by the sad ending of the pantheonic Howie Morenz, an ice poet whose glory once convinced the builders to put ice in Madison Square Garden, and who died of a broken heart when he realized he'd never play hockey again.

With the people come events, resonating beyond the walls of the arena to become symbolic. When an English-Canadian National Hockey League president banished the francophone god Maurice "Rocket" Richard from the 1955 Stanley Cup playoffs, the subsequent riot caused $100,000 in damage to Montreal, but was less about vandalizing a street than about venting centuries of French anger at the English. Indeed, some cultural observers have called the Richard Riot the flash point for Quebec nationalism that began in 1960, and which so occupies Canada's national imagination today.

In remembering hockey's defining moments, my emphasis falls on the professional North American game's evolution, because the pro arena is the measuring standard, and hockey's story on this continent has been, until quite recently, the world's dominant one. Dominant, too, is the keen relationship between technology and sport, for hockey's greatest moments have often become such because a camera looked in the right direction. While there were no cameras present when James Creighton staged his now-famous game, the fact that Montreal's *Gazette* advertised his experiment at all is due to the engineer Creighton's social standing at the Victoria Rink. If his had been an Irish and French squad playing on the frozen St. Lawrence River, the papers might not have had space for him.

In subsequent generations, much of what we love about this poetic, violent, fast, gloriously improvisational sport has been formed by our memory of images. That famous photo or that celebrated TV highlight have reached an iconic status that other moments might have reached, too, had they been caught by the camera. Even though the world's first professional hockey league, formed in Houghton, Michigan, in 1904, and the formation of the NHL in 1917, are defining moments, the cameras were not around to catch them, and so, in a visual book such as this, they are regrettably left behind.

The moments that have been chosen are both famous and not. They are moments that might be glorious or tragic or even prosaic, moments that have given hockey and us this passionate winter romance. They are moments that explain why we knock off work early to watch a team well out of the playoffs play its last game of the season, or rise with the bakers to watch an international contest live via satellite, or just strap on the skates (or roller blades) and go for a spin in that great imaginary rink, where you can be anyone and do anything, and write your own happy ending.

Hockey first began on a patch of ice, with blades made of animal bone and then of steel, with tree branches for sticks, and with frozen horse manure or a block of wood to knock toward the opponent's goal. The object of players then, and now, was joy— to feel the wind in their hair and their own defiance of gravity as they moved faster than any runner in a ball game could ever hope to, spraying ice into the crisp air as a kind of punctuation to their authority over a winter game. This book is also a testament to those who imagined, to those whose skill, vision, greed and genius were so authoritative that their names and deeds were indelibly etched in the ice, making possible all those moments of crushing sorrow and soaring ecstasy by which we colour life in winter.

WINNING THE FIRST STANLEY CUP

Sir Frederick Arthur Stanley arrived as Canada's sixth governor general in the spring of 1888 with no idea that he would change sporting history. Yet by the end of his first Canadian winter, Stanley had fallen in love with hockey, and on March 12, 1892, he gave the game a gift, proposing a new "challenge cup" to be held each year "by the leading hockey club in Canada."

Though other regional and league-based trophies already existed, Stanley's "Dominion Challenge Trophy" would have teams compete for it both home and away, creating regional rivalries in which the vast and sparse Canada—not yet 30 years old—could unite. Stanley commissioned a football-size silver alloy trophy from a London silversmith, one that cost him 10 guineas—then about 30 weeks' pay for the average London working man—and while that trophy is now priceless, the story of the "first" Stanley Cup champions is even richer in irony.

Montreal had become hockey's North American capital, with McGill University, the gentlemen's sporting clubs and the city's vivacious winter carnivals providing a

The Montreal Victorias' Graham Drinkwater chases the puck in a rare action photo from a game in 1895. Though hockey had been played in indoor rinks for two decades, the outdoor rink was at the heart of hockey life, breeding the players who would win glory indoors. Drinkwater and the Victorias would win the Stanley Cup later that year.

sophisticated social context for the game. The city also anchored the premier Amateur Hockey Association of Canada with three of its five teams: the Crystals, the Victorias and the Montreal Hockey Club.

Yet Ottawa boasted a four-team hockey league, and Stanley always hoped his beloved "Ottawas" would first win his Cup. The 1893 champion Ottawas thought so, too, but when they learned they would have to compete for it, they balked.

In the fall of 1893, Ottawa decided to play along, but lost to the Montreal Hockey Club, champions of the Amateur Hockey Association. So Montreal became the "first" Stanley Cup winner. But there was another problem: the team refused to accept the trophy. The Montreal Hockey Club resented the glory-sharing claimed by the Montreal Amateur Athletic Association, with whom it had "connected club" status but no voice in, and when the Cup was to be presented, the Hockey Club's chairman was "out of town."

The MAAA executive happily accepted the Cup for him, and the furious Hockey Club insisted the trophy be dispatched to the governor general, which the mortified MAAA saw as treason. So they kept it, and as their official history records, "the public

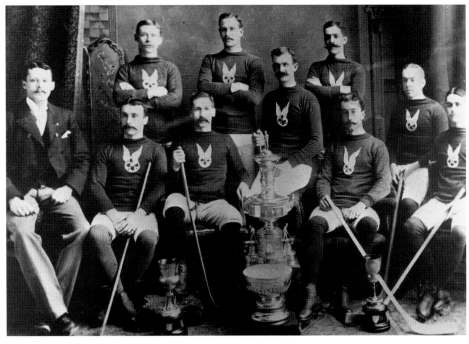

was never informed of the dispute." In fine Canadian tradition, the "first" Stanley Cup was won by a committee, in secret.

The first publicly resolved Stanley Cup series finally came to pass on March 22, 1894. Five thousand people crammed into Montreal's Victoria Rink to watch Ottawa and Montreal battle for what the *Gazette* reminded was not only "the Canadian championship, but the governor-general's cup." Women wore ribbons showing their loyalties—blue for Montreal, red for Ottawa—and Montreal won the spirited end-to-end match 3–1.

The champs were carried on the shoulders of their delighted fans, and the names of the "first" Stanley Cup champions were duly engraved in history: Tom Paton, James Stewart, Allan Cameron, Alex Irving, Haviland Routh, Archie Hodgson, G. S. Lowe, Bill Barlow and A. B. Kingan. Though the little silver bowl would grow huge in the winter hopes and dreams of the world's hockey fans and major corporations, and its pursuit would shape the way hockey evolved, one last irony remains: Lord Stanley sailed for England before that "first" historic match was finally played, and never saw his trophy awarded.

WANTED!
Quartz & Placer Claims
BY
A.J. BANNERMAN & CO.
MINE BROKERS
GENERAL AGENTS
POST OFFICE

THE DAWSON CITY
CHALLENGE

Less than a decade into its existence, the Stanley Cup had become hockey's defining icon, and the 1905 Dawson City Nuggets wanted to prove just how good they were by winning it. In the end, their epic quest for his lordship's silver in the dead of winter would prove a singular test of endurance that changed the challenge rules for hockey's most vaunted prize.

The Yukoners wanted to take the Cup from the Ottawa Hockey Club, a team led by the patrician Frank "One-Eyed" McGee, a goal-scoring prodigy and the nephew of a Canadian Father of Confederation. The Ottawa squad was nicknamed "the Silver Seven," a sobriquet that reflected early hockey's extra position of rover, and the fact that the club's delighted directors paid the team in seven shiny silver nuggets to honour its first Stanley Cup triumph in 1903.

The only thing lustrous about the Dawson City Nuggets were their dreams. Composed of civil servants, aging ex-players and one teenager, the Nuggets were the invention of one of Canada's most swashbuckling characters—Joseph Whiteside Boyle, a Woodstock, Ontario, native and now a Yukon entrepreneur.

Dawson City at the height of the gold rush was filled with adventurers, all hoping to strike the mother lode. On public holidays such as this one in the summer of 1898 or 1899, the town came out to celebrate with racing, gambling and thirst-quenching, fuelling the kind of dreams that made Dawson City confident to challenge for the Stanley Cup a few years later.

HOCKEY FEVER

(Above) The Ottawa "Silver Seven," one of hockey's finest teams, pose with another piece of silver in 1905. Led by "One-Eyed" Frank McGee *(standing, far right)*, the Silver Seven/Senators won 10 Stanley Cup challenges in all. Despite his impaired vision, McGee made it into the front lines of the Canadian army in World War I and was killed at the Somme in 1916. *(Right)* By the turn of the century, hockey was popular throughout Canada, with leagues and clubs for both men and women dotting the nation. In 1902 the North-West Mounted Police, responsible for keeping the peace in the often riotous Yukon, blew off steam by dressing as women for a "drag" game in Whitehorse.

Dawson City felt it had a chance, but first the team had to beat Mother Nature. On December 18–19, 1904, the players set out on dogsled and bicycle, but a sudden thaw forced them to walk. After battling a blizzard to Skagway, the team arrived in the Alaskan port to learn its ship had sailed. The Nuggets' next ship was trapped by ice for three days. Once the SS *Dolphin* had navigated the stomach-churning seas south, both Vancouver and Victoria were fogbound, so the Nuggets sailed to Seattle and made their way back to Vancouver on January 6, 1905, to catch the transcontinental train to Ottawa.

Seasick, battered and probably more than a little dispirited, Joe Boyle's team arrived in the capital on January 11, 1905—25 days after it set out. Newspapers across the country had chronicled the club's grand odyssey, and a huge crowd turned out to welcome it, but Ottawa refused the Nuggets' request for a brief postponement. Governor General Earl Grey would "face" the puck at 8:30 P.M. on Friday the 13th.

Despite the fact that the mighty Frank McGee could only put one puck past the Yukoners' teenage goalie Albert Forrest, the Silver Seven took the first game 9–2. One rash Klondiker dared to mock Frank McGee's single tally, and he responded in the next game with four goals in the first half and 10 in the second. In Ottawa's 23–2 pasting of Dawson City, McGee's 14 goals established a Stanley Cup record that still stands. The Silver Seven celebrated their massacre by hosting the victims to a lavish banquet, and then took their prize and drop-kicked it into the Rideau Canal, fortunately then frozen solid.

The Stanley Cup's trustees tightened the rules after Dawson City's remarkable challenge, so a team that wanted the "Jug" would have to prove its right to challenge. No more would an untested hockey crew make an epic transcontinental journey to face the best in the country—or in history. The mighty Silver Seven, later called the Senators, won 10 Stanley Cups in all, and in 1950 Canadian sports editors selected them Canada's greatest team in the first half of the 20th century.

TROPHY HUNTERS

It took the Dawson City Nuggets 25 gruelling days to reach Ottawa, but the team posing outside Ottawa's Dey's Arena on January 14, 1905, have put hardship well behind their severe game faces, taking their lead from Joe Boyle *(centre)* in their determination to avenge their 9–3 loss the night before and recoup the $10,000 the quest would cost.

INVENTING THE MONTREAL CANADIENS

Hockey and the Montreal Canadiens seem to be the kind of inseparable union that has descended from the gods: as long as there has been hockey in Quebec, there have been the Canadiens. It's a comforting thought, but the invention of the great francophone *bleu, blanc et rouge* was a plot cooked up by Irish Ontarians in the winter of 1909, and the reason, as usual, was money.

Thirty-five years after James Creighton's indoor hockey experiment in Montreal, the game had evolved into a sport, with paid players, competing leagues and a social structure that had enshrined the game as Canada's national winter obsession. Despite Montreal's historic importance to the evolution of hockey, a professional francophone team did not yet exist in the city.

Indeed, hockey had been largely the domain of Montreal's Anglo-Protestant ascendancy, and it was the city's Irish Catholic community that taught the francophones the game. However, Senator Michael O'Brien, a wealthy industrialist from the creamery town of Renfrew, Ontario, had no notion of conceiving the Montreal Canadiens in the winter of 1909 when he sent his 24-year-old son Ambrose to Montreal.

Nicknamed "The Flower" and *Le Demon Blond* to capture his artistry and desire, the Montreal Canadiens' Guy Lafleur slept in his hockey gear as a child; as a man, he dressed to play hours before the first face-off. With flying hair and hot eyes, *Le Demon* made the ice his heaven, winning three scoring titles, two regular-season and one playoff MVP awards, and five Stanley Cups.

13

(Left) "Little Giant" Aurele Joliat duels in front of the New York net in the 1930s. Though Joliat came to Montreal in an unpopular 1922 deal, the left winger's speed and élan made him a darling. One frustrated opponent grumbled that if Montreal moved Joliat to centre and held a mirror to each side of him, they'd have hockey's fastest line. *(Below, far left)* This 1911 Imperial Tobacco hockey card commemorates the Montreal Canadiens' Edouard "Newsy" Lalonde, one of the most colourful players ever to lace up skates. Lalonde won scoring championships in four different leagues, and took on all comers with his fists—even teammates. *(Below, near left)* The Montreal Canadiens of 1912–13 featured some of early hockey's greatest players. The legendary goalie Georges Vezina, discovered in a game in Chicoutimi the season before, sits between Newsy Lalonde and Jack Laviolette *(with dog)*, while defensive star Didier Pitre grins at the end of the bench. The Club Athlétique Canadien would not develop the distinctive CH crest on its sweaters until 1922.

Ambrose's mission was to ask the Eastern Canada Hockey Association to let Renfrew into its august body so that it could have a chance to win the Stanley Cup. Yet on November 25, 1909, the bosses of Montreal's Shamrocks and Wanderers, and those from Ottawa and Quebec, had other, weightier matters on their minds.

The Wanderers had been sold to J. P. Doran in 1908, and the wily Doran now proposed the team move to the smaller Jubilee rink—which he just happened to own—and which would shrink the 40 per cent share of profits the other owners took from one another's gate receipts. The owners solved their problem by dissolving their league to form a new one, the Canadian Hockey Association. And Doran and his Wanderers could have their tiny rink—because they weren't going to be in the new league.

Spouting curses, the Wanderers' furious forward and team official Jimmy Gardner stormed out of the meeting, clapped eyes on Ambrose O'Brien and had an idea. With the O'Briens' three-team league in Haileybury, Cobalt and Renfrew, plus the Wanderers and a French-Canadian team, there could be a new league, with the francophones appealing to the pocketbooks of their confreres.

On December 2, 1909, in the old St. Lawrence Hall in Montreal's St. James Street, the National Hockey Association was born. The francophones' team manager, Jack

Laviolette, proudly exclaimed that the new team would carry *"le nom de Canadien."* Even so, sniffed the anglophone *Gazette*, "French-Canadian players of class are not numerous."

Laviolette, a dashing defenceman who had once spirited big Didier Pitre south to play for the riches of the International Hockey League, now set about signing his talented friend. "Cannonball" Pitre had also signed a contract with the Montreal Nationals of the rival Canadian Hockey Association, and after much wrangling in the courts, he finally suited up for *Les Canadiens* on January 5, 1910, as they took on Cobalt.

After falling behind 4–0, Cobalt revived and took a 6–4 lead. But the Canadiens fought back. Art Bernier, "Skinner" Poulin and the feisty "Newsy" Lalonde each scored two goals, but it was Jack Laviolette—appropriately, after all he had been through to secure Pitre—who won the game in overtime for Montreal. Laviolette and

(Left) "Roadrunner" Yvan Cournoyer, only five foot seven and 178 pounds, blazed up and down the right wing for 15 years as a Hab, scoring 492 career goals and winning 10 Stanley Cups, four of them as the Canadiens' captain. Here both he and Jean Beliveau show the special frisson at scoring on the Toronto Maple Leafs' Johnny Bower. *(Below)* Nicknamed "The Lamplighter" for his talent at switching on the goal light, left winger Hector "Toe" Blake won the 1939 Art Ross Trophy as the NHL's leading scorer, and in the 1943 season became part of the fabulous Punch Line with Elmer Lach and Maurice Richard. Blake later coached the Canadiens to eight Stanley Cup titles before packing it in after losing the 1967 Cup to Toronto.

Pitre were the brightest stars in the firmament, and the duo played defence with such speedy élan that sportswriters would soon christen the team "the Flying Frenchmen."

The following season the Montreal Canadiens changed ownership when George Kennedy claimed rights to the name Club Athlétique Canadien and threatened an expensive lawsuit. The NHA granted him a new Canadiens franchise, to which he signed the "old" Canadiens players, with their former franchise sold to Toronto to become, irony of ironies, a forerunner of the Maple Leafs.

In 1916 the Canadiens won the first of 24 Stanley Cups, and over the next eight decades some of the most fabled names in hockey's pantheon would wear the team's red, white and blue. Known affectionately as "Les Habs," a diminutive of *les habitants*—or "the inhabitants"—the Club de Hockey Canadien would come to define what a championship tradition meant and win their other nickname, *les glorieux*.

THE MILLIONAIRES' STANLEY CUP

It was an ambitious dream, bringing professional hockey and artificial ice to North America's Pacific coast, but in December 1911, that's exactly what Lester Patrick and his younger brother Frank planned to do. When the Vancouver Millionaires did the unthinkable and won the Stanley Cup four years later, it made the Patricks look like geniuses. Which, of course, they were.

The patriarchs of "Hockey's Royal Family," Lester and Frank Patrick combined visionary innovation and cold-eyed practicality. The brothers learned their hockey in Quebec, playing shinny on Montreal rinks with the likes of future Hall of Famer Art Ross. Lester was one of hockey's first rushing defencemen who defied the convention of dump-and-chase. By 1907 the 24-year-old had won two successive Stanley Cups with the Montreal Wanderers, while 22-year-old Frank captained the McGill Varsity squad.

The Patrick brothers also played in the high-salaried National Hockey Association in Renfrew, Ontario, and made tours to the artificial ice palaces in the United States. When their father Joe sold his lumber business in booming British Columbia for $440,000, he had a fortune he wanted to spend.

Frank Patrick, the innovative genius of hockey's "Royal Family," was also a defenceman of note, setting a record with six goals in a Pacific Coast Hockey League game in 1912. Despite his administrative duties as the league's first president, and as manager and coach of the Vancouver Millionaires, he played on and off in his league until 1925.

Practical Lester thought their father should keep his money in his pocket; visionary Frank remembered New York City's St. Nicholas Rink and how it packed in thousands to watch hockey on fake ice. So he convinced his father to bet the family fortune on artificial ice arenas in a region of mild winters, and surprisingly, Joe Patrick agreed.

The Patricks' Pacific Coast Hockey League was born on December 11, 1907, with teams in Vancouver, Victoria and New Westminster. For $27,000 Joe Patrick bought land overlooking Vancouver's Coal Harbour and North Shore mountains, then built an artificial ice palace costing $275,000. With a capacity of 10,500, the Vancouver Arena was the largest indoor rink in the world, bigger than Madison Square Garden.

Frank Patrick, 26, became the Pacific Coast League's president and managed and coached Vancouver, while Lester, 28, ran the show in Victoria. Soon the brothers picked up eastern stars like the Montreal Canadiens' "Newsy" Lalonde, and Frank Patrick suited up on defence and set a record for the new league by scoring six goals in one game.

Frank then turned his attention to 27-year-old Fred "Cyclone" Taylor, the man for whom he coined the term *superstar*. The younger Patrick's offer to make Taylor hockey's highest-paid player at $1,800 a season convinced him to head west and won the new league greater legitimacy.

The Patricks also reinvented hockey, introducing numbered jerseys, the penalty shot and line substitutions. They allowed goalies to fall down to make a save, and they divided the ice into three zones, bisected by "blue" lines 67 feet apart. To open up the game they permitted forward passing in this middle zone, still forbidden in the east.

By 1915 the Vancouver Millionaires were ready to crown the experiment when they played the Ottawa Senators in the first Stanley Cup match staged west of Winnipeg. Sea level conspired with balmy springtime to make the Senators sluggish, and the Millionaires delighted 7,000 fans with a 6–2 win. In the next match, Cyclone Taylor potted three goals of his own, while gifted Frank Nighbor added two for Vancouver's 8–3 win. The final match was a blowout, with Vancouver's Barney Stanley scoring four goals and Mickey MacKay and Nighbor each adding three in the Millionaires' 12–3 win.

Only four years after starting their Pacific Coast League, the Patricks had won the game's top prize. They had also sold their New Westminster team to Portland and would soon put one in Seattle, where in 1917 the Metropolitans would become the first American team to win the Stanley Cup. Though the world's first pro league was born in Houghton, Michigan, in 1904, and the one that would endure would be born in Montreal as the NHL in 1917, the Patrick's expansive, innovative and daring adventure on the Pacific had truly made hockey the sport of a continent.

MILLIONAIRES ALL

(Far left) With its 10,500 capacity, the Vancouver Arena was the world's largest indoor rink, bigger by 500 seats than Madison Square Garden. *(Inset)* Lester Patrick had won two Stanley Cups as a defenceman with the Montreal Wanderers and was a highly paid star in the National Hockey Association before he and his brother Frank brought hockey to the Pacific Ocean in 1911. *(Above)* Led by the bowler-hatted genius of Frank Patrick, the Vancouver Millionaires topped the Pacific League and won the 1915 Stanley Cup.

THE DEATH OF
HOBEY BAKER

He was the kind of athlete who brought sophisticated Manhattanites to their feet when he touched the puck, a man whom women wanted and men wanted to be, and who moved F. Scott Fitzgerald to distil his essence into fiction, appropriately, in *This Side of Paradise.* Hobart Amory Hare Baker, hockey's first American-born "superstar," symbolized a generation whose innocence would be eviscerated on the killing fields of World War I, and he died as heroes often do—too young.

Hobey Baker learned hockey at the elite St. Paul's School in Concord, New Hampshire, often practising alone into the night, understanding how to feel the puck when he couldn't see it. In 1910 he entered Princeton, and though he became the All-American football captain, hockey was his favourite sport. Playing rover, he would circle his net two or three times to gain momentum for a goal-to-goal rush as the crowd rose screaming, "Here he comes!" His patrician Philadelphia lineage, athletic gifts and natural humility moved fellow Princetonian Fitzgerald to admit: "He was an ideal worthy of everything in my enthusiastic admiration . . . "

Since Princeton didn't have its own arena, the Tigers played their "home" games at New York City's St. Nicholas Rink. The marquee boasted "Hobey Baker Plays

In aerial combat, Lieutenant Hobey Baker found the exhilaration and speed he had loved on the ice, and called the clouds his "ice fields." When Baker was promoted to captain of the 141st Pursuit Group, the planes of his squadron were decorated in the orange and black colours of Princeton, with a tiger standing over a spiked German helmet painted on each fuselage.

Here Tonight," and his rich fans' waiting limousines stretched for blocks. When he graduated from Princeton in 1914, Baker left behind a legacy of 27 hockey wins and seven losses. However, his postgraduation Wall Street job with J. P. Morgan bored him senseless, so he sought release with the St. Nicholas Rink's elite amateur hockey team, five of whom had their own valets.

After the St. Nicholas team played the Montreal Stars for the Ross Cup on December 11, 1915, the Pacific Coast Hockey League's Lester Patrick enthused that Baker could have starred in his first game of professional hockey. Baker was even offered $3,500 to turn pro in Canada, but he only played for love, and refused.

Still craving the pure glory of his college years, he went off to war, joining the Escadrille Lafayette in April 1918. He shot down an enemy plane at Ypres that May and won France's Croix de Guerre for "exceptional valour under fire." Captain Hobey Baker was promoted to command the new 141st Pursuit Group, and though he was two kills short of the five that made an "ace," his unofficial total ominously numbered 13.

When the war to end all wars finally staggered to a conclusion on November 11, 1918, Baker pleaded to remain in France but was refused. On a cold, rainy December 21, 1918, though, he decided to take "one last flight." He discovered a recently repaired plane, and despite vigorous protests from his ground crew, he took it up. Baker had just levelled off a quarter of a mile from the base when the plane's engine cut out. Not wanting to ditch the aircraft, Hobey tried to impose his will on the machine to make it fly. He failed, and died in the arms of his comrades, aged 26.

It was long rumoured that the magnificent Hobey—the only man to win places in both the College Football Hall of Fame and the Hockey Hall of Fame—had committed suicide rather than return to a life of relentless anticlimax. He did not, but rather, tried to win just one more time, and on their front pages newspapers across America tolled the passing of a symbol. "Hobey Baker," lamented a headline, "Was America's Ideal Athlete."

THE PRINCETON TIGER

Hobey Baker's fellow Princetonians
regarded him as out of this world.
"With his wavy blond hair, his flashing
blue-grey eyes and straight features he
was as handsome as a Greek God,"
said one contemporary. "In height he
was about five foot nine, and I don't
believe he ever exceeded in weight
160 pounds. He was one of those
athletes who are never hurt."

FOSTER HEWITT'S
FIRST BROADCAST

On the evening of March 23, 1923, a young *Toronto Star* employee who broadcast Toronto Symphony concerts for CFCA, the newspaper's radio station, was sent to Toronto's Mutual Street Arena two hours before game time. His mission was to broadcast a hockey playoff game between the amateur teams representing Parkdale and Kitchener, an assignment no one else wanted. Using a telephone as a microphone, and constantly interrupted by both telephone operators and the nagging feeling that no one could hear him, the young man was about to change the social landscape for generations of hockey fans.

Foster Hewitt was well aware going into that historic game that he didn't know anything: nobody knew how to broadcast a hockey game and he certainly hadn't spent the first 21 years of his life practising play-by-play commentary. "I sat hunched on a small stool, in a small glass box . . . about four feet high," he later shuddered. "The air inside was warm, while outside the rink was cold, so the glass became so fogged the players seemed to be floating on clouds. For 60 minutes I talked, sweated and window-cleaned. I couldn't wait for the game to end."

Foster Hewitt's trademark "He shoots, he scores" came in a variety of modulations. When calling a goal for the Leafs on the road, Hewitt said he almost had to speak like an undertaker, but when the crowd noise swelled for the home team, Hewitt was at its mercy, having to shout out the news above the din.

THE VOICE

(Top) Up in his broadcast gondola,
Foster Hewitt shouted, "He shoots,
he scores!" as airborne Toronto
defenceman Bill Barilko's shot hit
the mesh behind Montreal Canadiens
goalie Gerry McNeil to win the 1951
Stanley Cup in overtime in Game 7.
(Bottom) It was the greatest
comeback in Stanley Cup history,
and Hewitt called out its exciting climax
to North America, and to Canadian
soldiers overseas in April 1942.
Down three games to none against
the Detroit Red Wings, the Leafs defied
the odds and the skeptics to win the
next four, and the Stanley Cup.

Later, when the formidable Conn Smythe was drawing up plans for Maple Leaf
Gardens at the beginning of the Great Depression, he asked Hewitt where the broadcast booth should be. The young sportscaster responded by climbing the stairs of the
new Eaton's department store building at College and Yonge Streets to gaze down at
pedestrians, gauging the best vantage point for his eye on hockey. When he found the
height that allowed him a wide perspective and still the ability to pick out pencils in
pockets, he was sold.

Hewitt's crackly, excited cadence cut through the darkness of the Depression, and
those sitting next to the wireless in Moose Jaw, Victoria, Sherbrooke, St. John's, or

Detroit could connect to a wider world of magic that cost only a trip to one's imagination. His familiar greeting of "Hello Canada and hockey fans in the United States and Newfoundland" added "an extra big hello to Canadian servicemen everywhere" during World War II.

The Voice also imprinted itself on young boys who dreamed of one day suiting up in the big leagues so people could hear Hewitt rhapsodize about them. The redoubtable Bobby Hull, Hall of Fame sniper for the Chicago Black Hawks and Winnipeg Jets, once confessed that when he first met the diminutive Hewitt, it was like "meeting God."

Hewitt made the transition from radio to TV, and so came into the consciousness of another generation who watched the *Hockey Night in Canada* broadcasts and thrilled to the sounds of his expert play-by-play. As a man who believed his broadcasts provided a crucial psychological link in the national drama, he came out of retirement at the age of 70 to call the historic Canada–Soviet Series in 1972, and once again Canadian hockey fans' hearts moved with his authoritative, emotional rhythm. Even the Soviets recognized hockey's pioneering broadcast voice and referred to their own august play-by-play man as "Russia's Foster Hewitt." And all because of an obscure amateur hockey broadcast assignment in Toronto 49 years earlier.

CANADA WINS WINTER OLYMPIC GOLD

By 1924 the Olympic Games had come back with a vigour appropriate to its motto of *citius, altius, fortius.* The Great War had suspended the competition in 1916, as the sporting event seemed incompatible with world war. Now a robust group of male amateurs carried the banner for Canada to Chamonix, France, at the first Winter Games in 1924 (the Winnipeg Falcons won Canada's initial Olympic hockey gold at the Summer Games in Antwerp in 1920). The Toronto Granites were the national team, having won the Ontario Hockey Association Championships in 1920, 1922 and 1923, and even more impressively, back-to-back Allan Cups—the Holy Grail of amateur hockey.

The team played its first game under the snowcapped peaks of Mont Blanc on January 28, 1924. Cheered on by W. A. Hewitt, sports editor of the *Toronto Star* and father of Foster, as well as coach Frank Rankin, former star of the Eaton's Hockey Association, the Canadians made short work of Czechoslovakia. Led by Reginald "Hooley" Smith, who would later star with the Montreal Maroons, and Harry

The Whitby Dunlops, a Senior A Ontario team, outmuscle the Soviets in a 1957 game at Maple Leaf Gardens, which they won 7–2. The following year, the Dunlops had outscored their opponents 78–4 by the time they met the Soviets again, beating them 4–2 to win the 1958 world tournament final.

"Moose" Watson, called "one of the greatest amateur hockey players to tear up and
down a left wing," the Canadians gave the stunned Czechs a 30–0 pasting they would
never forget.

The next day the Canadians beat Sweden 20–0, and on the third day of the tournament they embarrassed the Swiss 33–0, with Moose Watson scoring 14 goals. In the
team's gold-medal match against the United States, Watson was knocked out cold 20
seconds after the opening face-off, but came back to score a hat trick in the Canadians' 6–1 triumph. By the end of the carnage, Canada had scored 110 goals and allowed
only three in five matches.

In Paris the victorious Canadians were wined and dined at chic Claridge's Hotel;
in London on St. Valentine's Day, the grateful nation feted the champions at a dance
at British Columbia House on elegant Regent Street; and the Prince of Wales himself,
the future Edward VIII, invited them to pop by for a glass of champagne at St. James
Palace, just down the road.

When Moose Watson returned to Canada, the wooing continued as professional clubs bombarded him with offers. The Montreal Maroons—a team created for the Montreal anglophone community in 1924—offered Watson a staggering $30,000, twice the amount that James Strachan and Donat Raymond had paid the NHL for their franchise. Watson responded to Mammon's overtures by retiring for seven years, then returned in glory to play for and coach the strictly amateur 1932 Toronto Nationals to another Allan Cup.

Canada's Olympic golden hockey fortunes would continue with the University of Toronto Grads in 1928, the Winnipeg Hockey Club in 1932 and, after World War II, the RCAF Flyers and Edmonton Mercurys. Though a powerhouse for the first half of the century, Canada has since watched other countries rise to the gold on the podium. Despite the great hopes at the 1998 Winter Games in Nagano, Japan, when NHL professionals went to reclaim the nation's Olympic heritage, Canada hasn't won an Olympic hockey gold medal since 1952.

ARYAN OLYMPICS

The 1936 Winter Olympics, held at Garmisch-Partenkirchen, Germany, were a showcase for Nazi supermen and hosted by Adolf Hitler himself. Under sunny skies in an outdoor rink, the Canadian goalie casts a sunglassed eye on the puck in a match against the United States. Canada would take silver; a team of Canadians representing Britain would win gold.

CONN SMYTHE BUILDS
MAPLE LEAF
GARDENS

A talented hockey player, a fearless soldier wounded in both the First and Second World Wars, a gambler, a philanthropist, a bully and a hockey genius, Conn Smythe was one of the game's most contrary greats. As the man who invented the Toronto Maple Leafs and built them a home in the midst of the Great Depression, he is the creator of "(English) Canada's Team," and the founder of one of hockey's greatest shrines: Maple Leaf Gardens.

In 1926, when George "Tex" Rickard saw the New York Americans succeed in the new Madison Square Garden he helped build, he wanted a team, too, and 31-year-old Conn Smythe, coach of the University of Toronto Varsity squad, was the man to get him one. Smythe's amateur hockey had taken him to out-of-the-way places, and he created the New York Rangers by plucking from obscurity future stars such as goalie Lorne Chabot, the brothers Bill and "Bun" Cook and centre Frank Boucher, all for only $32,000.

The insular pro hockey world, though, sneered that Smythe's Rangers were just a bunch of amateurs, and the Rangers' president, Colonel John Hammond, stung by

Despite the crushing Depression, Conn Smythe wanted a building in which he could make his Leafs "Canada's Team." Eaton's department store offered land at the corner of Toronto's Church and Carlton Streets for $350,000 and a stock option; workers took shares in lieu of cash, and Maple Leaf Gardens was built in less than six months.

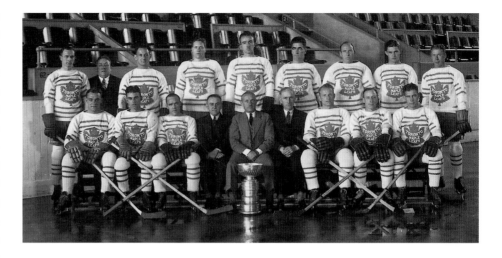

ARCHITECT OF DREAMS

(Top right) Five years after Conn Smythe promised revenge on the New York Rangers, his Leafs defeated them to win the 1932 Stanley Cup.

(Below left) Smythe, in his University of Toronto sweater outside the city's old Mutual Street Arena, was a distinguished alumnus, captaining the varsity hockey team that won the 1915 Ontario championships, then coaching the varsity seniors to the 1927 Allan Cup.

(Below right) Though he had once captained Upper Canada College's hockey team, Smythe *(seated, extreme right)* "hated" the aristocratic private school and in 1910 transferred to Toronto's Jarvis Collegiate, aged 15.

this suggestion, fired Smythe shortly before the team's debut, withholding $2,500 of his $10,000 salary.

In one of those fateful turns that always seem to colour history's epic characters, Smythe went to the Rangers' opener against the Montreal Maroons as a guest of Tex Rickard. When the Rangers won, an ecstatic Rickard offered Smythe a job as vice president. With characteristic "diplomacy," Smythe blustered that he wouldn't take another breath for those "cheapskates," then told Rickard how he had been cheated.

Rickard made good on the outstanding $2,500—half a year's salary for a top-notch player—and Smythe prudently invested it in a college football game, doubling his money. When the Rangers went to play the Toronto St. Pats, Smythe got five-to-one odds on the winning Rangers, and in three days made $10,000. He found investors to front the rest of the St. Pats' $160,000 sale price, and in 1927 he, too, had a team.

The bigoted Smythe thought the name St. Patricks was too Irish Catholic for his taste, so he dressed the team in University of Toronto colours, renamed it the Maple Leafs and promised the "blue and white" would win the Stanley Cup within five years.

Smythe then built a contender with top players such as Irvine "Ace" Bailey,

Clarence "Happy" Day, Joe Primeau, Lorne Chabot, Harold "Baldy" Cotton, Reginald "Red" Horner, Charlie Conacher and Harvey "Busher" Jackson. But Smythe thought his team needed one more ingredient—the irrepressible Francis Michael Clancy, who said he would suit up for Hell before he would skate for the loathsome Leafs. But Clancy's cash-strapped Ottawa Senators offered him for $35,000, and Conn Smythe turned to gambling once more, winning enough money on a horse race to buy "King" Clancy.

Then Smythe set out to erect a palace. On June 1, 1931, after many delays, the ground was finally broken for Maple Leaf Gardens. A mere five months later the Leafs lost their first game in the new arena to Chicago, but made it to the 1932 Stanley Cup finals, where they swept the New York Rangers. Almost five years to the day that Conn Smythe had promised to wreak revenge on the traitorous Rangers by winning the Stanley Cup within five years, he and his team did so in Maple Leaf Gardens.

KING OF THE HEELS
Francis Michael "King" Clancy was the man Conn Smythe needed to win the Stanley Cup. Clancy's father, a rugby football star in 1890s Ottawa, was so expert at heeling the ball out of the scrum that he was called "King of the Heelers." Clancy Junior joked that he was just "King of the Heels," but his splendid hockey playing won him the nickname "King."

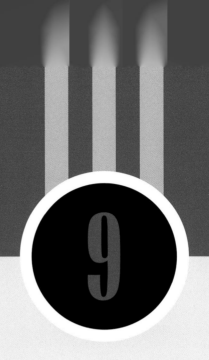

THE SUDDEN END OF
HOWIE MORENZ

The scruffy kids, the sobbing matrons, the hard hockey men holding back tears, and the 50,000 mourners who passed his casket in the Montreal Forum believed a god had died. A quarter million more bowed their heads to his cortege in March 1937, suspecting they would be dead, too, before the ice ever saw the blades of Howie Morenz's equal.

He was the most unlikely of heroes. As a child, he scalded his legs so badly it was thought he'd never walk again, let alone become the fastest man in the fastest game. When summoned to the pros by the Montreal Canadiens, he didn't want to leave his amateur stardom in Stratford, Ontario, so he returned his $850 signing bonus. Montreal, unmoved, told him he would play for them, or not at all.

On his first shift on Boxing Day 1923 against Ottawa, 22-year-old Morenz scored the first of his 270 goals, and three months later the Canadiens met the Calgary Tigers for the Stanley Cup. With his speedy wingers Billy Boucher and Aurele Joliat, Morenz's line accounted for eight of the Canadiens' nine goals over two games. The man who didn't want to play professional hockey wound up drinking champagne from the Cup in his first season.

Partway through the 1935–36 season, Howie Morenz, "the Stratford Streak," was traded from Chicago to New York. The lights of Broadway seemed to light up Morenz, bringing back some of his old magic in the city to which he'd brought the game of hockey a decade earlier. Yet when Cecil Hart called him back to Montreal for the 1936–37 season, the Stratford Streak was overjoyed.

(Above) On March 12, 1937, thousands of mourners packed the Montreal Forum to attend the funeral of Howie Morenz. Once, he had brought thousands to their feet in rhapsodic delight at his speed and daring, but on this day only grief and mourning black coloured Morenz's ice palace, making it a mausoleum. *(Below, far right)* Two days after his fibula was snapped above the ankle when he crashed into the boards in a game against Chicago, Morenz can't muster a smile for the camera. Despite the beer and whiskey brought by well-wishers and hidden beneath the bed to encourage conviviality, Morenz couldn't hide the despair that some say killed him a few weeks later.

Morenz became one of Montreal's great dandies, a clotheshorse who sometimes changed his suit three times a day, who played the ukulele and who made people laugh. When Montreal won, he was on top of the world, and when they lost, he took it as a family death.

Morenz often played far out of position and in a dream, but he could see the play before it happened, and pounced on the puck to speed it on goal to the rapture of a generation. However, despite his triumphs—three Stanley Cups, three Hart Trophies as National Hockey League MVP and two Art Ross Trophies as leading scorer—injury and excess caught up to Morenz. In 1932 the team he once spurned sent its prince into sorry exile in Chicago. When Morenz scored for the first time *against* his beloved Canadiens, the Montreal Forum patrons gave him a standing ovation—for him, and for their own nostalgia.

After another trade to the New York Rangers, Morenz's fortunes changed when Cecil Hart, under whom he had won two Stanley Cups, agreed to coach the Canadiens for the 1937 campaign on one condition: he wanted Howie Morenz back. And on the night of January 28, 1937, there he was, making improbable things happen between ice, steel, rubber and wood. When he broke through the Chicago defence to chase a loose puck, Black Hawk defenceman "Big Earl" Siebert chased him.

Morenz tripped, catching his skate in the boards. Siebert crashed into him, and the sound of Morenz's snapping leg echoed through the Montreal Forum like the

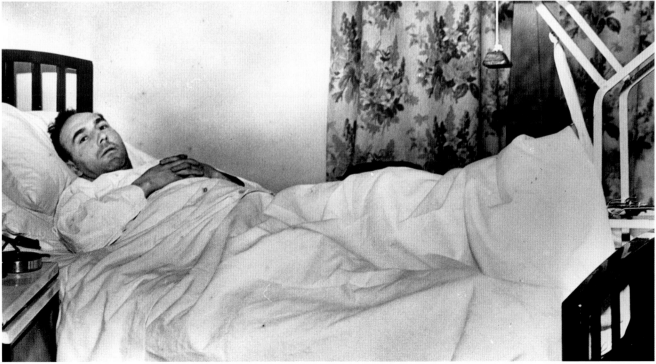

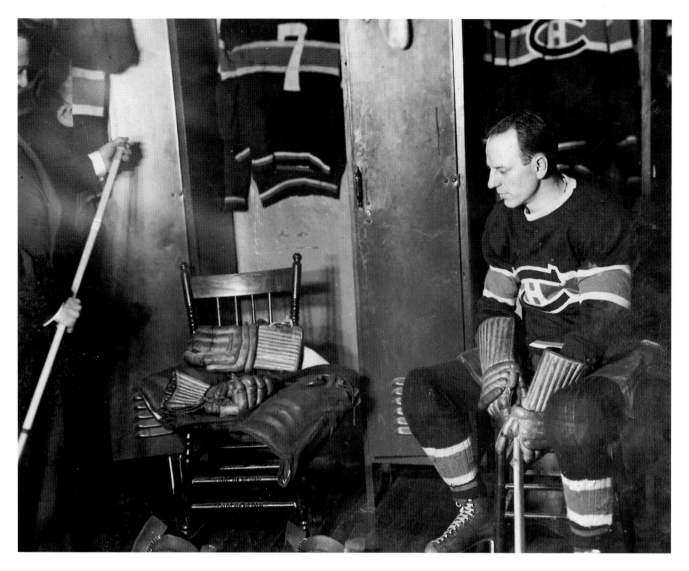

A SENSE OF LOSS

(Above) Aurele Joliat sits in distracted grief next to the stall of his dead linemate and hero, Howie Morenz. When Morenz came back to the Canadiens from New York in 1936, he rejoined his pal Joliat. *(Facing page)* Morenz, the once-reluctant Montreal Canadien, poses proudly in the uniform he came to define. In 1922 Morenz scored nine goals for Stratford, Ontario's Canadian National Railways team. The game's referee had played amateur hockey for the Canadiens' coach Cecil Hart, and called him with the news of Morenz's brilliance. Hart went to see for himself, and Montreal soon had a new icon.

shattering of a dream. From his hospital bed, Morenz joked with visiting players and drank prodigiously from a stash of whiskey. Yet he worried to his friend Joliat that he was done, and his high living had bankrupted his wife and children. Pointing to heaven, he said he'd watch the Canadiens win the Stanley Cup "from up there."

On March 8, 1937, Morenz died in his sleep at the age of 34, officially from a coronary embolism. Aurele Joliat saw it in more tragic terms: "Howie loved to play hockey more than anyone ever loved anything, and when he realized that he would never play again . . . Howie died of a broken heart."

The Canadiens held a benefit game for Morenz's family, and collections of $20,000 were put into trust, yet low interest rates kept annual payments at $600. A year after Howie died, one of his daughters succumbed to pneumonia, and his widow Mary, only 29, broke down. Howie Junior and his surviving sister were placed in an orphanage.

The tragedy of Howie Morenz's young death, and the destruction of his family, mirrored the social devastation of the Depression and revealed pro hockey's inability to look after its own. Even so, when Canadian Press sportswriters voted in 1950 on hockey's greatest star of the first half of the century, "Cyclone" Taylor won three votes, "Rocket" Richard, four, and Morenz, 27. The man called the greatest player ever had won his last prize from his grave.

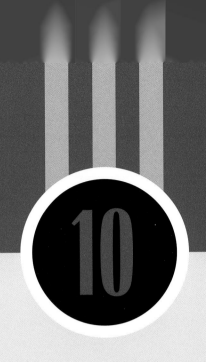

QUEENS OF THE ICE
REIGN SUPREME

From 1930 to 1939, Ontario's Preston Rivulettes won big, amassing 10 regional championships and six national titles, tying three times and losing only twice in their 350 games. When their dynasty ended in 1941, it wasn't due to the rise of another, but to war. Gasoline was rationed and money was tight, and a women's hockey team—no matter how good—wasn't deemed essential to the war effort.

Women had been playing hockey for as long as men, despite frequent disapproval. When a 1894 Queen's University women's team in Kingston, Ontario, drew the ire of the local archbishop, who felt its challenge to a men's team to be the first blast of the apocalyptic trumpet, the suitably chastened women wittily called themselves the "Love-Me-Littles" and played on.

Women's hockey leagues sprang up across Canada, with teams representing everyone from civil servants to secretaries to universities. The social codes for female modesty were such that some ladies' teams played their matches in rinks safely protected from any male eyes, other than those of the referee. In deference to delicate

It was a long time coming—more than a century after Lord Stanley's daughter Isobel played on a Government House team against the Rideau Ladies in 1889—but in March 1990 the world's best met in Ottawa in the world's first women's hockey championship. Team Canada's Susana Yuen is hoisted by her mates in celebration of Canada's 5–2 win over the United States.

PEERLESS CHAMPIONS

Such was the fame of the Preston
Rivulettes that they were invited
to stage a European tour, one
prevented by World War II. Though the
women's Dominion Championship
disappeared in 1940, and the
Rivulettes disbanded the following year
due to wartime rationing, they were
elected to the Canadian Sports Hall of
Fame in 1963 as the greatest
women's hockey team yet seen.

public sensitivities that could withstand bloody mayhem in men's hockey but might swoon at a female leg, the women played in long skirts, which they used to tactical advantage. Goalies spread their skirts along the goal line to stop the puck, while forwards took advantage of their billowing modesty to conceal the puck.

In 1900 the first women's league was stocked by three teams from Montreal, Trois-Rivières and Quebec, and the first money-making women's matches were staged in Montreal when the Quebec Society charged admission to a women's game to aid wives of Canadian soldiers fighting in the Boer War.

The Preston Rivulettes, ironically, began life as a softball team, and decided in 1930 that they needed a new challenge, so they took up hockey. Led by forwards Hilda Ranscombe and Marm Schmuck, and backstopped by Nellie Ranscombe, the Rivulettes, by 1932, won the Ladies' Ontario Hockey Association's intermediate

WOMEN OF THE ICE

(Left) The Dawson City "Dawsons" pose with the "Victorias" in the Dawson Athletic Association rink in 1904. *(Below)* The Buffalo Snow Birds hockey team brave a 1920s winter to play a little bathing-suit shinny. Women's hockey had once been constrained by social mores that deemed a naked calf provocative, but the freedoms of the Jazz Age changed that.

league, and moved up to the senior division, where they easily handled more experienced teams. That March they took on the Edmonton Rustlers for the first Dominion Women's Hockey Championship title.

After a long and expensive train journey from Ontario, the tired Rivulettes were shocked when the Rustlers handed them their first-ever loss, winning 3–2, and repeating the score in the second game—the only losses the Rivulettes would suffer. The 2,000 spectators who turned out saw a tough, skilled series that further buoyed the popularity of the women's game, and cinemagoers the following week could see newsreel highlights of women's hockey, putting the women's game on an entertainment level with the men's.

Throughout their career, the Rivulettes and other women's hockey teams were hard-pressed to meet travelling and equipment expenses, and the Great Depression only added to the misery. When the Rivulettes beat the mighty Montreal (women's) Maroons in 1936, only 168 fans turned out, leaving the Rivulettes with $150 less in anticipated gate receipts, and the indignity of paying $5 a woman to their "host" Maroons for provisions at their postgame victory "party."

The Rivulettes continued their domination of women's hockey up to the beginning of World War II, and were about to embark on a European tour when war cancelled the trip. Finally, in 1941, the team disbanded, unable to raise travel money in times of rationing. There were no expensive plans to save them as there would be with the New York Americans and Rangers a few months later, and their passing was not mourned in the streets.

After the war, women's hockey languished in the attitude that women should be watching, not doing, but resurged in the 1960s spirit of emancipation. In 1990 Canada won the first official women's world hockey championships, and by 1998 the Canadians and Americans had worked themselves into a great hockey rivalry that culminated in the U.S. women beating Canada for the gold medal at the Nagano Olympic Games. Even though the Preston Rivulettes had been absent for 57 years, their achievement on the ice was reflected in those glittering women's hockey medals at Nagano.

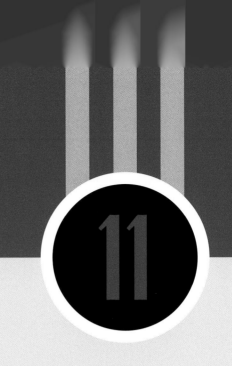

ROCKET RICHARD
SCORES 50 GOALS
IN 50 GAMES

On March 18, 1945, Montreal's 23-year-old scoring prodigy Maurice Richard did the impossible, and with a drama suiting his fiery persona. Once he'd beaten ex-Canadien Joe Malone's record of 45 goals (set over 22 games in 1918) by blasting a bad-angled one-timer past Toronto's Frank McCool, Richard still had eight games to reach the magical height: 50 goals in 50 games. Yet he couldn't get past 49. Finally, at 17:54 of the last period of the last game of the season, Richard scooped up a pass from Elmer Lach and fired it into Boston's net to set a mark that would endure for more than three decades.

As the second eldest of seven in a working-class North Montreal family, the first Canadiens game Richard ever saw was the first one he played in. Though ankle and wrist fractures often sidelined him in minor hockey and in his initial game as a pro, Richard took off on a mission to the stars in Game 2 of the 1944 Stanley Cup final against the Toronto Maple Leafs, the Canadiens' archenemies. By then Coach Dick Irvin had already teamed him up with Elmer Lach and Hector "Toe" Blake to form the legendary Punch Line.

On the ice, Maurice "Rocket" Richard's eyes were those of a great predator, terrifying goalies as he sought out another kill. Upon seeing his first hockey game in 1955 between Montreal and New York, the great American novelist William Faulkner said Richard possessed "the passionate glittering fatal alien quality of snakes."

Not yet tagged "the Rocket," Richard scored two goals 17 seconds apart in the first two minutes of the game, and fired his third before the period ended. In the third, he scored twice more to tie "Newsy" Lalonde's 1919 Stanley Cup record: five goals in one game. With the final score 5–1 for Richard against Toronto, broadcaster Foster Hewitt picked the three stars: "Maurice Richard, Maurice Richard and Maurice Richard."

Only five foot ten and 160 pounds, Richard could still carry 200-pound defence-men on his back but was cursed with weak bones. Even so, this flaw increased his potency as a political symbol. By the spring of 1944, 90 NHL players had signed up for the war, though the league wanted its marquee names kept safe. Stars such as Boston's Milt Schmidt were sent to England as player-coaches for the Canadian Bomber Group squad, and many Montreal Canadiens, including Richard, worked in

(Left) Maurice Richard fires one of his 626 career goals past Toronto's Turk Broda. The philosopher Marshall McLuhan wrote in *Understanding Media* that the Rocket "used to comment on the poor acoustics of some arenas. He felt that the puck off his stick rode the roar of the crowd." (Below) The Punch Line of Maurice Richard, Elmer Lach, and Hector "Toe" Blake spray ice chips circa 1946. Blake won the 1939 Ross and Hart Trophies, while centreman Elmer Lach nabbed scoring titles in 1945 and 1948, and the 1945 MVP award. With the explosive Hart winner Richard, the line formed one of hockey's most potent trios.

home front munitions factories, something English Canadians scorned as a sop to French-Canadian resentment at being forced to fight an "English" war in 1914. Nevertheless, the Rocket had indeed tried to enlist, but was twice rejected because of his fragile bones, so he waged his battles on the ice.

After Richard's amazing 1944–45 season, Toronto's Conn Smythe, who had never had a French-Canadian player on his team, and once began a speech "Ladies, gentlemen and Frenchmen," offered the Canadiens $25,000 for the Rocket, but he wouldn't leave Montreal, where he ranked a notch below the pope. Though Richard would spend another 15 seasons in the NHL, he never again scored 50 goals in any one of them. Still, it wasn't until 1981 that New York Islander Mike Bossy equalled the Rocket's magnificent 50-goals-in-50-games feat.

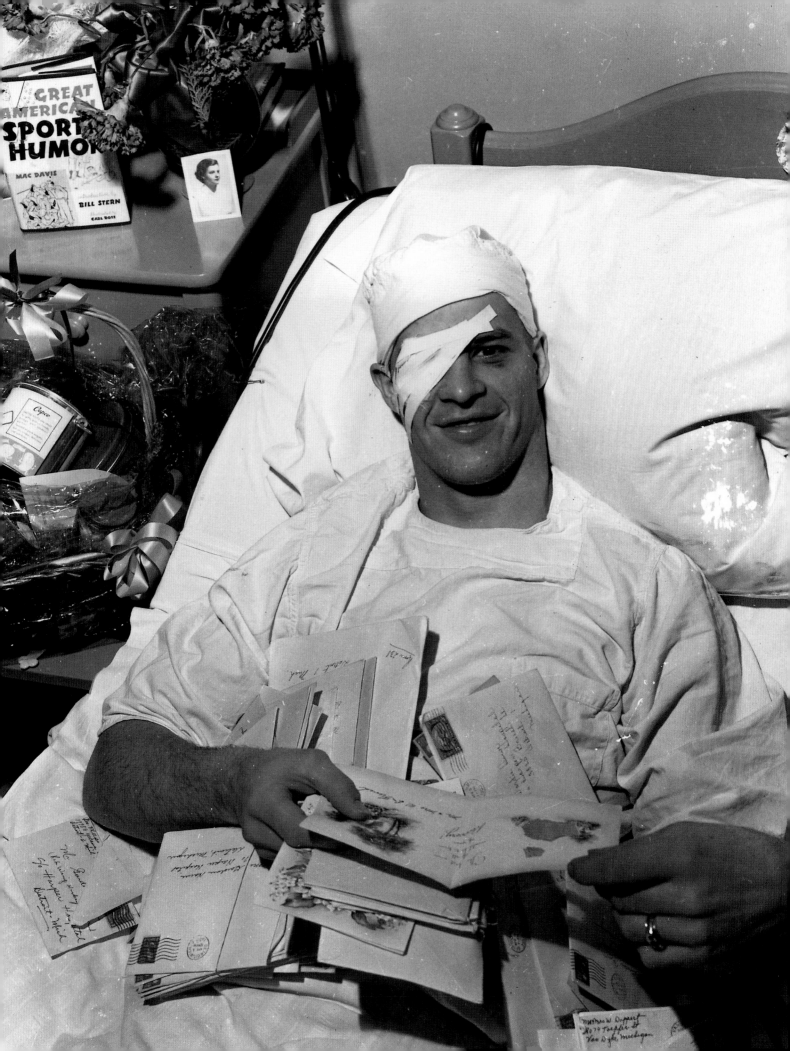

GORDIE HOWE
ALMOST DIES

A conceit beloved of fiction writers and day-dreamers alike is to posit the great "what if x never happened?" and then spin a new world from the missing event. What if Kennedy had never been shot? What if Columbus had stayed put in the Old World? What if the Detroit Red Wings' Gordie Howe had died on the night of March 28, 1950?

When Howe was carried unconscious from the Detroit Olympia, fans feared that the big right winger was going to die just three days before his 22nd birthday. Rumours even swirled around Detroit that Howe *was* dead, and sucked into the grave with him went a lifetime that even the most ardent fan couldn't have imagined: six Art Ross Trophies as the NHL's leading scorer; six Hart Trophies as the most valuable player; 21 selections to NHL All-Star teams; the MVP award in the World Hockey Association; the Lester Patrick Trophy for service to hockey in the United States; four Stanley Cups; the record for NHL points—1,850 over 26 seasons—until a kid named Wayne Gretzky caught him; and the sobriquet "Mr. Hockey," one earned over 33 seasons as a pro, and with unparalleled skill and ferocity.

Eight days after his terrible injury, Gordie Howe is able to smile amid his flood of sympathy mail. Indeed, Howe never lost his sense of humour during the ordeal, recalling later that he was conscious when the surgeons drilled into his skull to relieve pressure on his brain. "I was a little concerned there," he said. "I didn't know where they were going to stop."

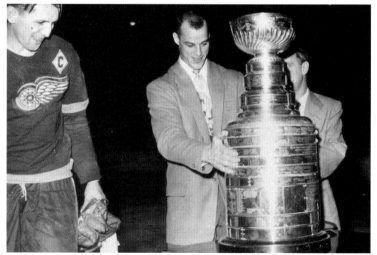

(Left) Gordie Howe raises one of his famous elbows as he goes after a loose puck, while Maple Leaf captain George Armstrong thinks twice about following him. Howe built his elbow technique into his skating style, so that a well-placed blow to an opponent's head innocently looked like part of his arm motion as he skated. *(Below, far left)* At the beginning of the 1950–51 season, Howe wore a leather helmet to protect a head badly injured only months earlier. But the future "Mr. Hockey" wanted to prove his injuries had done no harm to his skill and determination as a player, so he abandoned the helmet as soon as he could. *(Below, near left)* Almost fatally injured one month earlier, Howe touches his first Stanley Cup as if it were the Holy Grail. Years later he would explain that, because his injuries kept him out of the finals, he felt the Cup was not yet his. "I like to earn things," he said. "To be on the ice, and sweat and bleed with the boys."

No, all a fan would have known is that the Red Wings' great hope and glory had been badly hurt in the very first game of the Stanley Cup semifinals. Midway through the second period the league-leading Wings were losing 3–0 to their scourges, the Toronto Maple Leafs, when Gordie Howe aimed his six-foot frame and 200 pounds of might at Toronto's Ted Kennedy.

What happened is still debated. Kennedy says that Howe tripped, while Howe maintains that Kennedy's stick flew up, just as another Leaf player accidentally clipped Howe on the edge of his right eye. The Red Wing crumpled and slammed his head into the oak hardwood boards as blood gushed onto the ice.

Howe's nose and cheekbone were smashed, his eyeball was scratched, he had a concussion, and he had possible brain damage. He spent his 22nd birthday under an oxygen tent in a Detroit hospital, the prognosis for his recovery uncertain. And after losing both the "Big Guy" and the first game, the Red Wings literally took to arms, fighting two savage brawls that propelled them into the Stanley Cup finals.

MANUFACTURING GOALS

Hockey's fabled Production Line takes a break during practice. "Old Bootnose" Sid Abel *(right)* served as the line's foreman, cooling down Ted Lindsay and heating up Howe. The veteran Abel once claimed that he was only playing out of charity to keep young Howe and Lindsay in the league. "If it weren't for me," he joked, "they'd be in Indianapolis."

The New York Rangers hadn't played in a Stanley Cup final since their president burned Madison Square Garden's mortgage in the Cup in 1940, and they put up a fierce fight. With the game still tied 3–3 at 8:31 of the second overtime period of Game 7, Detroit's George Gee won a face-off in the New York zone and passed the puck to Pete Babando. His backhand shot from 15 feet out sailed into the top left corner of the net, and the Red Wings had won the Stanley Cup—their first since 1943.

The Olympia shook with emotion when Gordie Howe, a soft fedora on his head, came on the ice to celebrate with his teammates. Ted Lindsay, who with Sid Abel and Howe formed the Motor City's prolific Production Line, gently removed the hat so the crowd could see Howe's awful scars. "I'll never forget the night he came back, more so than the night he got hurt," Abel remembered. "The night we won it he got a standing ovation. We were all thrilled."

Gordie Howe recovered from his head injuries well enough to play in all 70 of Detroit's regular-season games the following year, scoring 43 goals and adding 43 assists to win his first Art Ross Trophy. For the next 22 years, Howe never scored fewer than 23 goals per season, and two years after retiring from Detroit in 1971, he joined sons Marty and Mark on the Houston Aeros of the World Hockey Association. At the age of 46, Mr. Hockey won the league's most valuable player award.

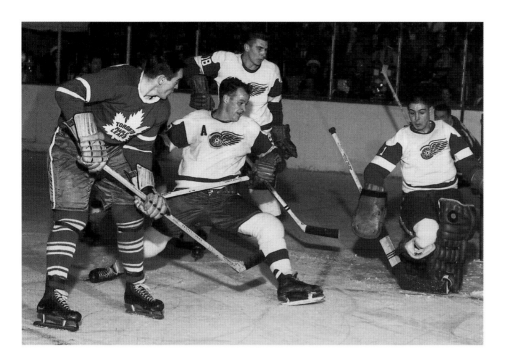

TWO-FISTED WONDER

(Left) Phenomenally strong, Gordie Howe was able to palm 90-pound sacks of cement while working on his father Ab's road crew. Such exercise built the kind of strength necessary to fend off the likes of Toronto's Frank Mahovlich and allow goalie Terry Sawchuk to control the puck. *(Below)* Howe puts one of his 869 NHL career goals past Toronto's Johnny Bower in a penalty shot on December 31, 1961. Able to shoot either left or right, young Gordie honed his technique by breaking shingles off the Howe family roof in July, and practised firing them both left- and right-handed.

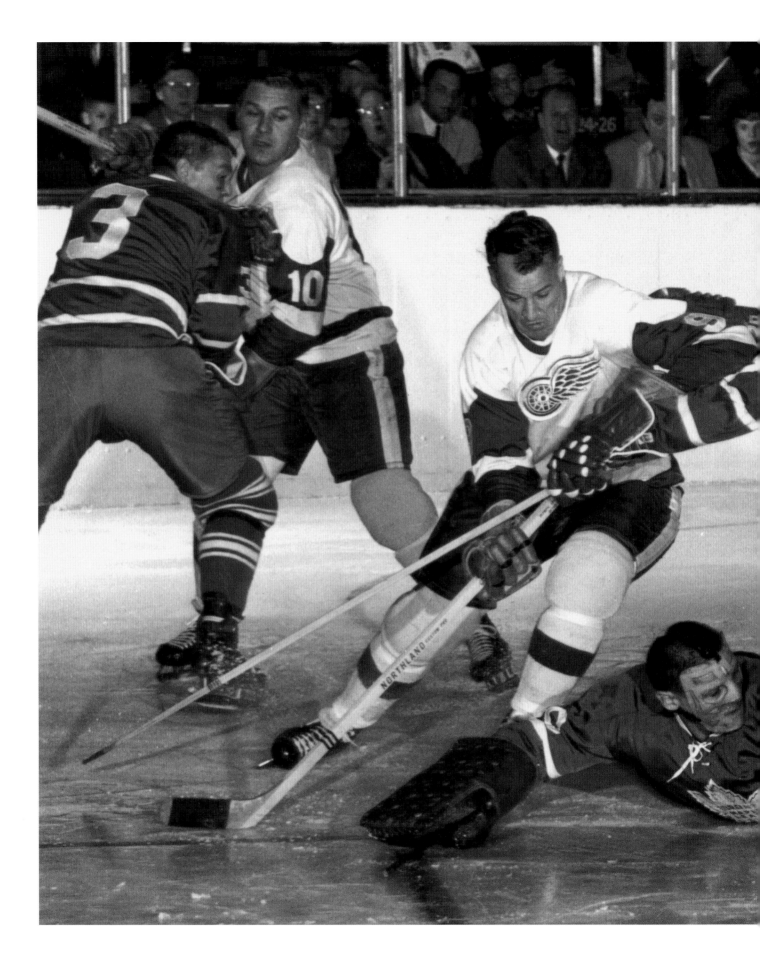

Gordie Howe fought some of his
toughest battles against the Toronto
Maple Leafs yet, ironically, could
have become one. Conn Smythe's
assistant, Frank Selke, discovered that
the teenage Howe—then playing in
Omaha, Nebraska—wasn't properly
registered as Detroit property. Instead
of stealing the young star for the
Leafs, Selke alerted his good friend
Jack Adams, and the Wings' coach
and general manager corrected what
might have been one of hockey's
greatest mistakes.

HOCKEY NIGHT IN CANADA MAKES ITS TELEVISION DEBUT

The first televised hockey game hit the airwaves in 1940 in New York City, only 17 years after Foster Hewitt's pioneering on radio. A decade later, television had so invaded the cultural consciousness of the continent that the Chicago Black Hawks became the first team to try out weekend matinee games in 1952, fearing that hockey couldn't compete with weekend night TV. So the Canadian Broadcasting Corporation decided to create the best of both worlds by putting hockey on television on Saturday nights, and *Hockey Night in Canada* became a winter tradition for generations of Canadian hockey fans, along with their American counterparts in the border states.

The network's first hockey telecast took place in Toronto on March 21, 1951, but only six people saw a show transmitted to a TV in the radio control room of Maple Leaf Gardens. Foster Hewitt did the first-period play-by-play, then resumed his radio broadcast. The initial CBC network telecast took place in Montreal on October 11, 1952, when Gilbert Renaud, a 24-year-old newspaper sports editor who hadn't even seen television, produced a hockey game between Montreal and Toronto.

Imperial Oil purchased the television rights to the first season of Toronto Maple Leaf games on *Hockey Night in Canada* for $7,000—or only $100 a game—since Leaf owner Conn Smythe wanted to gauge TV's worth before setting his real price. The following season Imperial Oil forked out $150,000 a year for three years, beginning the "Esso Tradition."

HOT STOVE NIGHTS

During the early years of hockey radio broadcasts, people would congregate around the hot stove at the local general store on winter nights to listen to Foster Hewitt on the "wireless." *Hockey Night in Canada* fuelled the intermissions of televised games with the wisdom and gossip of old-time players, coaches and hockey writers, giving TV viewers the sense that no matter where they lived, they, too, were part of the "Hot Stove League."

As televised hockey quickly supplanted radio as the advertisers' medium of choice, Canadian NHL clubs earned vaults of money, which they refused to share with their brethren in the United States until 1962. In 1963, when the U.S. network CBS planned to broadcast hockey on weekend afternoons after the football games had ended, the NHL was opposed, arguing that this would create too many travel and scheduling problems. The real reason was that it might create media stars out of lowly puck chasers who would start demanding their fair share of hockey's superlative revenues.

Now, in an age of televised pucks trailing blue and red comet trails, of afternoon playoff games in glorious springtime, and of an NHL increasingly anxious about its telegenic appeal in hockey hotbeds like Phoenix and Miami, *Hockey Night in Canada* seems like some unearthly innocent that managed to survive despite the commercial rigours of television.

With its cast of provocative characters on both the English and French telecasts, with its folksy geezers talking shop as if they were down at the Legion Hall, the show is what Foster Hewitt's radio broadcasts once were—a psychological link in what is still a vast and cold country. In francophone bars in Montreal, patrons switch to the English telecast when Don Cherry comes on to explain the nation to itself; in Saskatchewan, people brave the deep freeze of winter to stage garage parties around cases of brew and the TV hockey game; and in Vancouver, many a domestic Saturday night social calendar is torn asunder by televised hockey stretching from 4:30 in the afternoon to 90 minutes south of midnight.

Though some have argued that the constraints of television can never truly serve the speed and invention of hockey, the show has become the national stage for the national opera, putting us all in the front row to witness what this week's fate has in store for our cunning villains and swaggering heroes as they play out their dramas under the bright lights of one of our last reassuring cultural constants— *Hockey Night in Canada.*

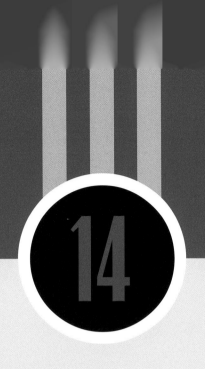

JEAN BELIVEAU SIGNS WITH MONTREAL

In 1952 Jean Beliveau was famous throughout Quebec, first as the star centre of the Quebec Citadels and then of the Aces. Nicknamed *Le Gros Bill* because of his six-foot-three, 205-pound stature and resemblance to a heroic character in a French-Canadian folk song, Beliveau beggared superlatives. The Montreal Canadiens, no strangers to the power of icons, knew that this 21-year-old could become the regal symbol of the *bleu, blanc et rouge* and bring them years of championship glory, but for one small snag: Beliveau didn't want to play for them.

Young Beliveau lived for hockey. After Sunday mass in Victoriaville, Quebec, he would race to imitate the exploits of Montreal's scoring prodigies "Toe" Blake and Elmer Lach on the backyard rink. During his stellar junior career, Beliveau rejected the Canadiens' pleas to join them, saying that Quebec City felt closer to home and that he liked the team's owner, Frank Byrne, a powerful figure in Quebec's pulp and paper industry.

Beliveau again rejected the Canadiens when he signed with the Quebec Aces, a senior pro team. The people of Quebec loved Beliveau, and merchants gave him suits and free steak lunches every time he scored three goals. Since the Canadiens owned

Jean Beliveau was adored in Quebec City, with merchants giving him suits and hats every time he scored three goals, and female admirers giving the handsome Ace something to laugh about. Montreal offered Beliveau a contract similar to Maurice Richard's $53,000 over three years. Beliveau, making more in Quebec, said, *"Non, merci,"* and stayed with the Aces until 1953.

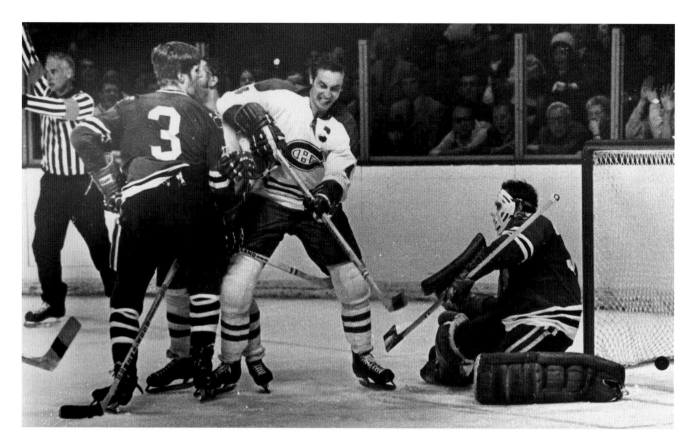

GALLANTRY AND GRIT

Jean Beliveau racks up one of his
97 playoff assists on a goal by Frank
Mahovlich in the third 1971 Stanley
Cup finals game against Chicago.
The Canadiens would go on to
win the series, and Beliveau would
sip champagne from his last of
10 Stanley Cups, retiring at the end
of the playoffs.

Beliveau's NHL rights, they called him up for a three-game "lend lease." Beliveau scored five goals, including a hat trick against the Rangers, and the Canadiens' general manager, Frank Selke, offered him a Rocket Richard kind of contract: $53,000 over three years. Beliveau, already making more in Quebec, went back to the Aces.

Though the Canadiens had won the 1953 Stanley Cup, the club's owner, Senator Donat Raymond, had seen enough, and bought the entire Quebec Senior Hockey League, thus turning it—and Beliveau—professional. The senator then told Frank Selke to put Beliveau in a Canadiens jersey once and for all. Newly married, Beliveau finally signed his Canadiens contract on October 3, 1953, while coach Dick Irvin flashed the victory sign.

Beliveau's contract weighed in at a guaranteed $110,000 over five years, the largest in the Canadiens' history, and the treasure himself played on a line with Rocket Richard and Bert Olmstead, a spirited left winger. Two seasons later Beliveau won the Art Ross Trophy as the NHL's leading scorer, and the first of his two Hart Trophies. Over his 18 seasons as a Canadien, Jean Beliveau would add another Hart and 10 All-Star selections and become the first man to win the Conn Smythe Trophy in 1965 as the most valuable player in the Stanley Cup playoffs.

Beliveau sipped champagne from the Cup 10 times, five of them as the Canadiens' captain. With his gift for seeing the play before it developed, his ability to stickhandle the puck as if it were part of his blade, and his beguiling mixture of toughness and elegance on ice, Beliveau defined not only the proud aesthetic of the Montreal Canadiens, but that of the country. In 1994 the 63-year-old eminence was offered an astonishing laurel for a hockey player: the chair once held by Lord Stanley. With customary grace, Jean Beliveau declined the job as Canada's governor general. After all, he was already a king.

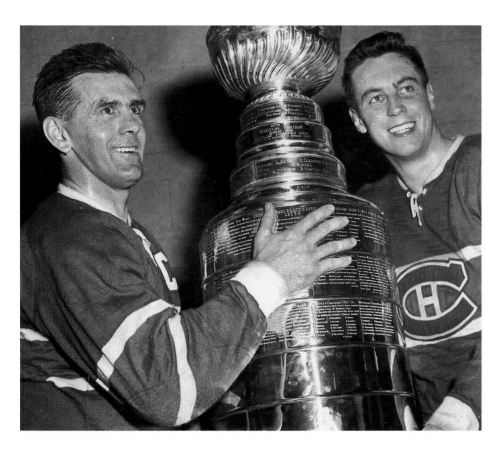

ELEGANT FIRE

(Left) An old Canadien icon and a new one greet their third straight Stanley Cup in 1958. When Jean Beliveau was signed by Montreal in 1953, he would pick up the torch that Maurice Richard would one day inevitably hand over. From 1956 through 1960, the Canadiens won five Stanley Cups in a row—a feat yet to be repeated. *(Below)* Captain Jean Beliveau celebrates—with Coca-Cola—another Canadiens triumph with *(left to right)* Henri Richard, John Ferguson and Yvan Cournoyer. With his winning mixture of grace and hardheadedness, Beliveau was worshipped by his fellow players. After 18 regular seasons with Montreal, *Le Gros Bill* made his elegance and excellence synonymous with that of the Canadiens.

MONTREAL HIT BY
THE RICHARD RIOT

With his green eyes ablaze, Maurice "Rocket" Richard regularly battled mugging opponents as he sped in on their rattled goaltenders. Famously he would take his revenge with a goal, yet when the enemy cut him with a stick or a punch, Richard wielded the sword with such fury that by March 1955, his résumé included several game misconducts and a league-leading $2,500 in fines. After he tussled with officials in Toronto, NHL President Clarence Campbell warned Rocket that one more rampage meant exile.

With four games to go, Richard had his burning sights on his first Art Ross Trophy as the NHL's top point scorer, yet he knocked it out with a punch—one that rocked the country and one impossible today, for no player means as much as Rocket meant to Quebec. In Anglo-dominated Montreal, the French-Canadian Richard was "a flag" to his fellow Québécois, a *bleu, blanc et rouge* battle standard of glorious passion and talent, one flying higher and braver than anything Toronto or the Americans could hoist. Yet Richard was more than a symbol, for by shrugging off lesser, Anglo mortals as he rocketed toward glory, he made the Québécois' winter dreams come true.

At the end of the first period, a tear gas bomb exploded in the Montreal Forum, and while the crowd made for the exits, NHL president Clarence Campbell headed for the first-aid centre, where he consulted with the Montreal fire chief before sending a note to Detroit's general manager Jack Adams: "The game has been forfeited to Detroit."

NIGHT OF ANGER

(Left) On the night of March 17, 1955, enraged fans fled the tear gas billowing in the Forum and took the riot into the streets. In an attempt to prevent any more damage, Montreal's police set up a cordon. *(Below, far left)* Maurice Richard sits out his suspension and watches the first period of the fateful March 17 game. After the rioters had torn the city apart, Richard went on the radio to appeal for calm. "So that no further harm will be done," he said, "I would like to ask everyone to get behind the team and help the boys beat the Rangers and Detroit." *(Below, near left)* Angry Montreal fans protest NHL president Clarence Campbell's suspension of their hero.

On Sunday March 13, 1955, Rocket Richard smashed those dreams when he punched linesman Cliff Thomson during a stick fight with Boston's Hal Laycoe. Richard accused Thomson, a former Boston defenceman, of holding him down so Laycoe could sucker-punch him. President Campbell, a Rhodes scholar and lawyer, disagreed, banishing the working-class francophone for the season and, unthinkably, for the playoffs.

English "justice" had failed again, and furious Québécois scaldingly taunted Campbell that Richard would still be playing were he named Richardson. One cartoon showed Campbell's head on a platter, captioned "This is how we'd like to see him."

Despite police warnings, Campbell attended the Canadiens' St. Patrick's Day game against archrival Detroit. Near the end of the first period, a man punched Campbell several times before the police intervened; another man crushed two tomatoes against the president's chest.

Then a tear gas bomb exploded. The screaming crowd, eyes stinging, rushed for air as the Forum organist sardonically played "My Heart Cries Out for You." With only 250 police to contain 10,000 people spilling onto St. Catherine Street, the crowd became a mob, smashing windows, setting fires, and overturning cars until 3:00 A.M. Rocket himself went on the radio to restore calm. "I will take my punishment," he said, "and come back next year."

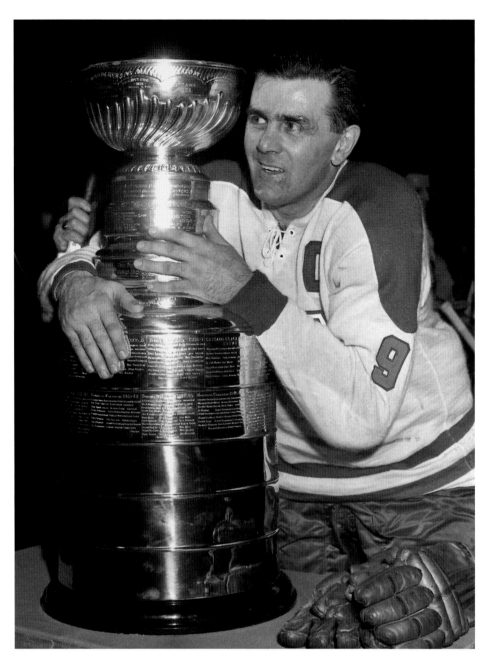

Though only 70 were arrested, the rioters cost Montreal $100,000 in damage. The broken windows hardly compared to the shattered Québécois hearts after 200 years of Anglo domination. Richard's injustice was *their* injustice, and front pages across North America shouted out their rage. Indeed, *L'affair Richard* has been called the flash point for Quebec's Quiet Revolution, a sometimes violent social conflict between French and English initiated in 1960 to define what Canada really means.

Hockey has since seen postgame melees of drunken malice, but never vengeance for a martyred hero, one who swore four decades later that the other NHL owners conspired to hustle him out of the playoffs. Five years after his riot, Richard bid hockey adieu, never closer to winning the scoring title than that tumultuous year when he lost it by one point. Still, Richard's stature as a cultural icon remained so profound that 23 years after he retired, Montreal's *La Presse* newspaper asked its readers to select the "man of the century." They chose folksinger Felix Leclerc, and the Rocket.

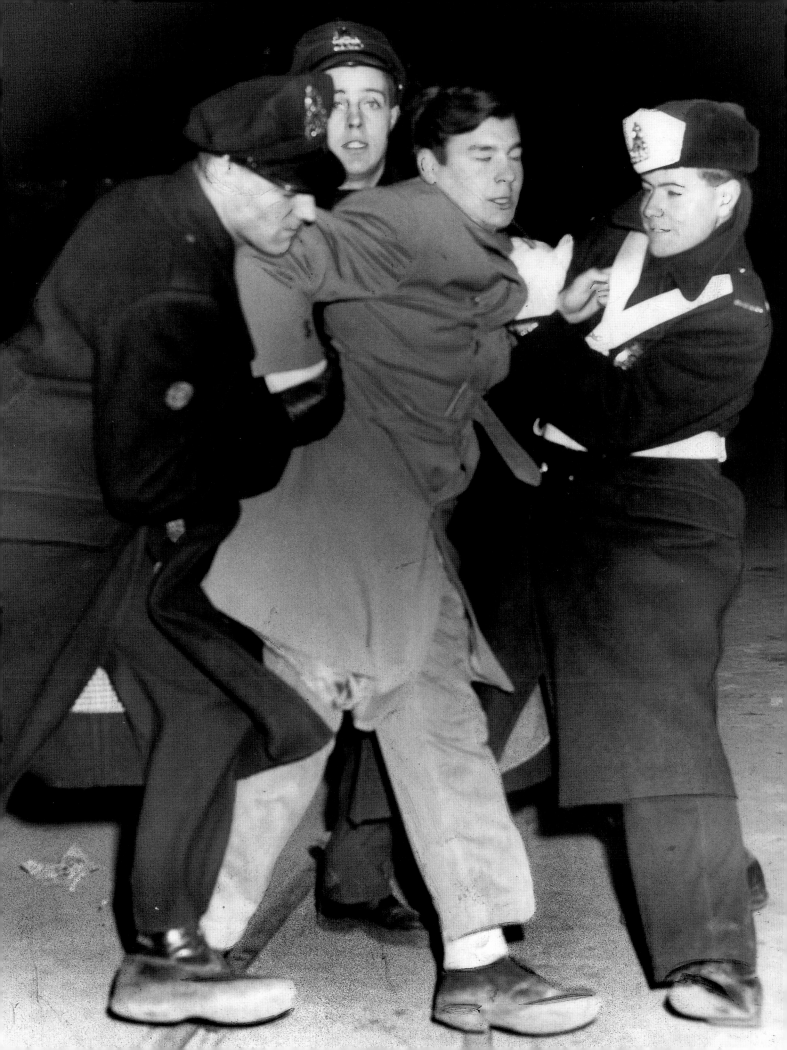

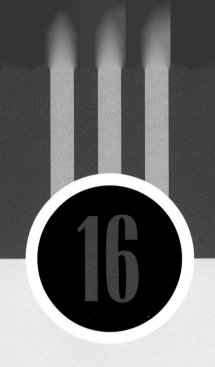

TED LINDSAY
IS TRADED TO
THE BLACK HAWKS

From 1949 to 1955, the Detroit Red Wings finished in first place every year, setting a record for professional sports teams. They also won four Stanley Cups and debuted players who would become legends: Ted Lindsay, Gordie Howe and Terry Sawchuk. On July 24, 1957, however, the Wings traded their 33-year-old former captain Ted Lindsay to the dreadful Chicago Black Hawks as punishment for daring to stand up to the NHL's tyranny.

Lindsay had led the NHL with 55 assists that year, and his 35 goals made his total the best by a left winger ever, to go along with his 1948 Art Ross Trophy as the league's leading scorer. Though just five foot eight and 160 pounds, "Terrible Ted" refused to back down from anyone.

When Lindsay was appointed in 1952 to the board of the NHL's Pension Society, he became frustrated by the NHL owners refusal to let the players see the books to their own pension fund—to which they contributed 20 per cent of their average $5,000 annual salaries, while the NHL kicked in $600 per man, and did so from revenues from the All-Star Game, which the players played in for free.

When Ted Lindsay was traded to the Chicago Black Hawks in 1957 as punishment for starting an NHL players' association, there was weeping and gnashing in Detroit, where he had been the feisty heart of the Detroit Red Wings. Typically Lindsay put on a brave face and continued his battles in Chicago.

THE SCRAPPER

Ted Lindsay battles around the Montreal Canadiens' net. Lindsay's tongue was as devastating as his play, and for years the Habs' Maurice Richard wouldn't speak to him, unable to forgive his shattering attacks with words. For Lindsay, it was all in a day's work: trying to win.

In 1956 Lindsay approached the Montreal Canadiens' defensive star Doug Harvey during a warm-up skate at the Forum. It was an act of singular courage, for Lindsay and Harvey had done their share of bloody sparring on ice, and interteam fraternization was forbidden by the NHL. Yet Harvey had served with Lindsay on the Pension Society board, and he agreed to the idea of a hockey players' association. Soon the duo had representatives from all six teams, and when they held a press conference in New York on February 12, 1957, to announce their association, they had signed up every player in the NHL except Toronto's Ted Kennedy, who was retiring.

Detroit boss Jack Adams put the fear of destitution into his team if they persisted, but Lindsay held firm. Adams responded by stripping Lindsay of his captaincy and degrading his performance to reporters while at the same time inflating his income to make him look like a greedy ingrate. Then he sent Lindsay packing to the basement in Chicago, along with fellow subversive Glenn Hall.

True to form, Lindsay held his own press conference, set the record straight about his salary and businesses, and then went to Chicago and continued his mission, filing an antitrust suit in October 1957 against the NHL owners' pro hockey monopoly. However, the Detroit Red Wings, led by Gordie Howe and "Red" Kelly who believed management's lies, resigned from this litigious tilt at the windmill, and soon the players' association was dead.

Lindsay would return to the Red Wings for one last season in 1964, and in 1977 he became the team's general manager. He remained rightfully bitter about the failure of the players' association, for had he won his war in 1957, there would have been no need for Alan Eagleson, the man who revived the players' association a decade later, and who used the players and their pension fund for his own criminal purpose.

TERRIBLE TED

(Left) Ted Lindsay was as bold around the net as he was everywhere else. Of his 379 goals, 57 were game winners, and when he retired in 1965, his 851 points were the highest total yet for a left winger. *(Below)* "Scarface" Lindsay soaks his badly bruised right knuckles after a fight with his foe "Wild Bill" Ezinicki in 1951.

JACQUES PLANTE
WEARS A MASK

On November 1, 1959, Jacques Plante's face met Andy Bathgate's thundering shot at Madison Square Gardens and goaltenders around the world were saved. Plante, the eccentric Montreal Canadiens goalie, had already won four of his seven Vezina Trophies as the NHL's premier backstopper, but refused to go back in goal unless armed against the New York Rangers' snipers.

His coach, Hector "Toe" Blake, agreed to let him wear a piece of gear that some had mocked as "sissy," and when Plante went back wearing a goalie mask, Montreal went on a 19-game unbeaten streak, which ended when he discarded the mask at Blake's urging. Chastened, the coach told Plante that if the face shield helped, he should wear it. Plante did, winning both his fifth straight Vezina Trophy *and* Stanley Cup.

Many hockey people thought that putting your naked face between a careening piece of frozen rubber and the scoresheet was just part of being a man—though hardly anyone knew the mask idea first came from a woman. In 1927 Queen's University goalie Elizabeth Graham wore a wire fencing mask to protect herself, and Montreal Maroons' goalie Clint Benedict had been the first pro to wear a mask in 1930, after his

A dazed and bloodied Jacques Plante dons the goalie mask that he designed himself. Though he had used the mask in practice, this marked the first time he wore it in an NHL game.

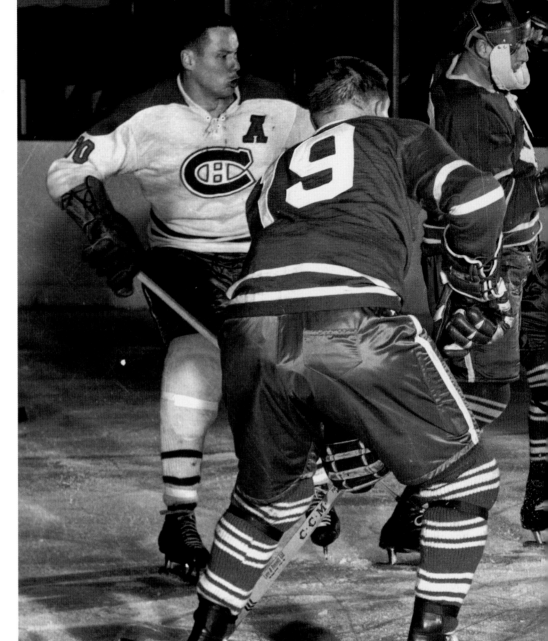

GOALPOST GUARDIAN

Jacques Plante leaves his net to poke-check an opponent. Even though Plante played behind some of the NHL's great defences, his own defensive skills were superb, picked up by necessity after he played on a junior team whose defencemen were often accused of secretly playing for the opposition.

nose had been broken that year by a Howie Morenz blast. Unfortunately Benedict's crude leather mask blocked his vision, and he abandoned it, then retired.

In 1955 Jacques Plante's right cheekbone was shattered by a shot from teammate Bert Olmstead, and he was out for five weeks. In 1956 a shot deflected into Plante's face, and while recuperating, he mentioned in a TV interview that he'd like to try out masks for goaltenders. A man in Granby, Quebec, sent Plante a plastic model, and he used it in practice for three years. In 1957 Bill Burchmore developed a fibreglass mask that could be moulded to fit the face, and he and Plante perfected it despite the objections of coach Blake, who thought it would make his goaltender complacent.

Jacques Plante was anything but. An extrovert who made mad dashes for the puck, yelled directions to his defencemen, fed forwards with long passes, and gave articulate bilingual postgame interviews, Plante kept to himself off ice, even checking into hotels

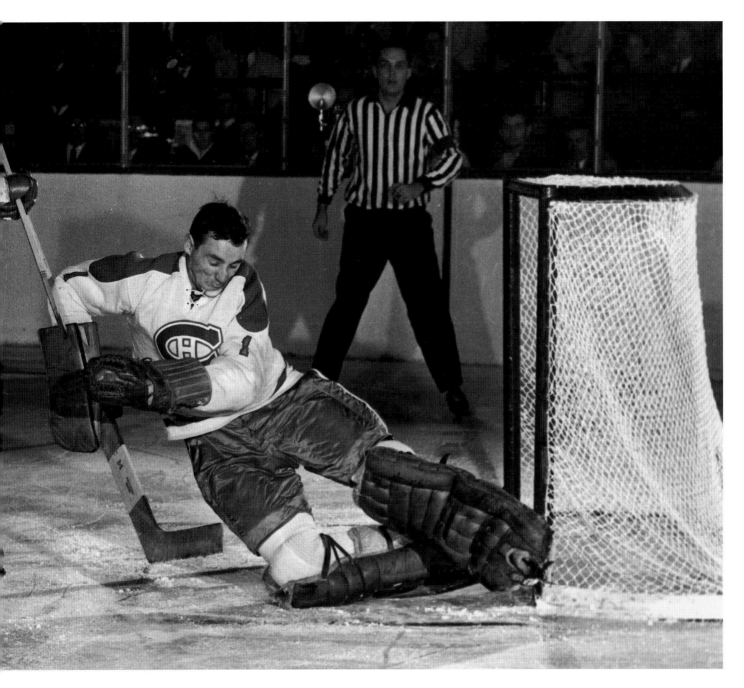

separate from the team on road trips. For relaxation he would knit toques and even his own underwear, and teammates called him cheap.

Plante had grown up devastatingly poor in Shawinigan, Quebec, and there was no money for a radio on which young Jacques could hear his Canadiens take flight. "I used to lie awake at night," he recalled, "listening to hockey games in the ceiling coming through from the radio upstairs."

He never dreamed that he would one day become known as goaltending's greatest innovator. Called "Jake the Snake" because he would make slithering dives to smother pucks, Plante's bold originality led to comparisons to Canada's piano genius, and he was called the "Glenn Gould of hockey."

Plante's flamboyant style was born of necessity as a junior with the Quebec Citadels, whose laggard and inept defencemen forced him to chase the puck out of self-

JAKE THE SNAKE

A premask Jacques Plante makes a save against an almost-masked Leaf. Plante was a true student of angles, and played them almost to perfection. If a player was going to score on "Jake the Snake," he was going to have to beat the rules of geometry.

TRIBAL MASKS

(Page 86) Montreal Maroon goalie Clint Benedict models his prototypical leather goalie mask in 1930.

(Page 87) Terry Sawchuk's 1964 mask *(upper left)* looks like an artifact from some lost civilization, while Gerry Cheevers's mask *(upper right)* featured painted stitches where pucks had hit him. In the 1970s, the mask became a canvas for the Gothic heraldry of Cleveland's Gilles Meloche *(lower left),* and by the 1990s, John Vanbiesbrouk's Florida Panthers helmet-cage "mask" *(lower right)* was both high protection mixed with tribal high style.

THE FIRST DOMINATOR

(Right) Jacques Plante's out-of-net-sorties were spectacular and effective. NHL owners punished him in 1959 by forbidding the goalie from falling on the puck outside the crease. *(Facing page)* The veteran Plante holds up his first mask, and his last. The protective gear helped him win seven Vezina Trophies as the NHL's best goalie, one Hart Trophy as the MVP, and six Stanley Cups.

preservation. This self-interested style came to dominate his long career, which ended in 1973 with the World Hockey Association's Edmonton Oilers when Plante was 46.

Yet when Plante donned his mask he not only lengthened his own career, but changed the way goalies played the game. The early mask—though still no guarantee against injury—evolved into a sophisticated shield that allowed netminders more freedom in how they chose to stop pucks. In the 1990s, it became a gaudy battle standard decorated with goalies' nicknames and intimidating images. Even so, the last maskless goalie to appear in an NHL game was Pittsburgh's Andy Brown on February 6, 1973. What Jacques Plante thought of that is captured by his response to those who questioned his masked manhood. "If I jumped out of a plane without a parachute," said Jake the Snake, "would that make me brave?"

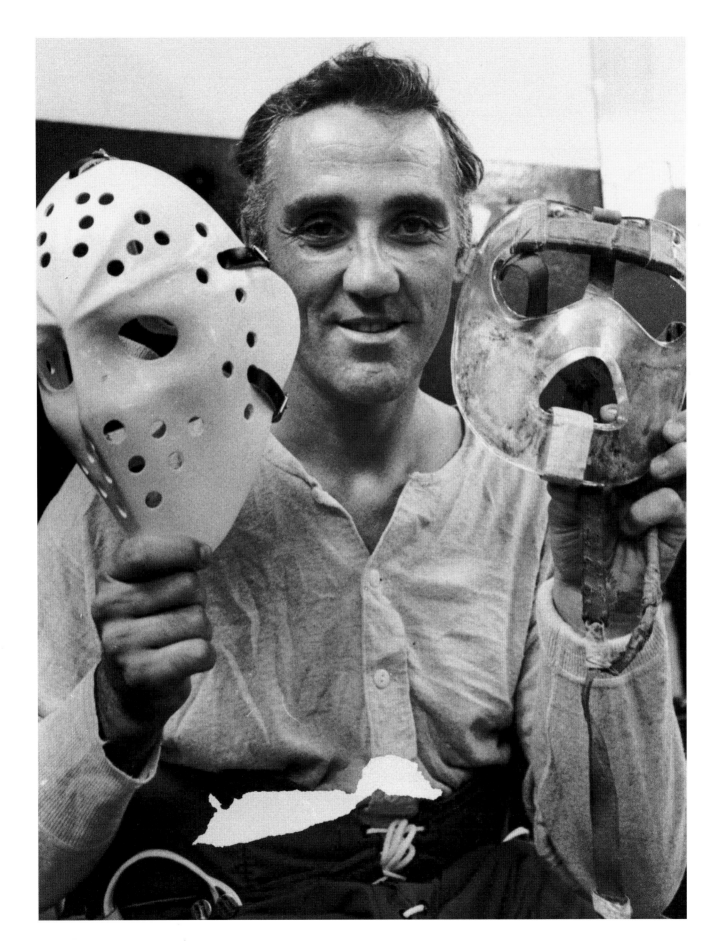

BOBBY ORR BECOMES A BOSTON BRUIN

For years he had been hymned as the messiah who would save a franchise that had won its last Stanley Cup in 1941, and that from 1960 through 1967 had finished dead last six times and second last twice. The Boston Bruins, however, knew that glory was on its way, for they had Bobby Orr, and he was mythic before he even pulled on a Boston sweater.

In 1960 Robert Gordon Orr was a five-foot-two, 110-pound, 12-year-old peewee playing in a tournament with 14-year-olds when Bruin scouts saw him and said the kid could have led Boston right then. In 1962 Bobby signed the standard NHL "C form," which gave Boston his hockey rights for life in exchange for $2,800, a second-hand car, and the promise of a new wardrobe, about which Boston forgot. The following year Orr's father met a young Toronto lawyer named Alan Eagleson, who was speaking at a sports banquet, and so began a relationship that would change the way hockey did business, as much as Orr changed the game he played.

In 1966·Orr turned professional, and Alan Eagleson represented the 18-year-old saviour. Bruin general manager "Hap" Emms sniffed that Boston wasn't prepared to

About the only thing Bobby Orr couldn't do was fly, but he does it here after scoring the winning goal in the 1970 Stanley Cup finals against St. Louis to bring the Bruins their first Cup since 1941. It is one of the most famous and symbolic photos in hockey history: Orr as winged victory.

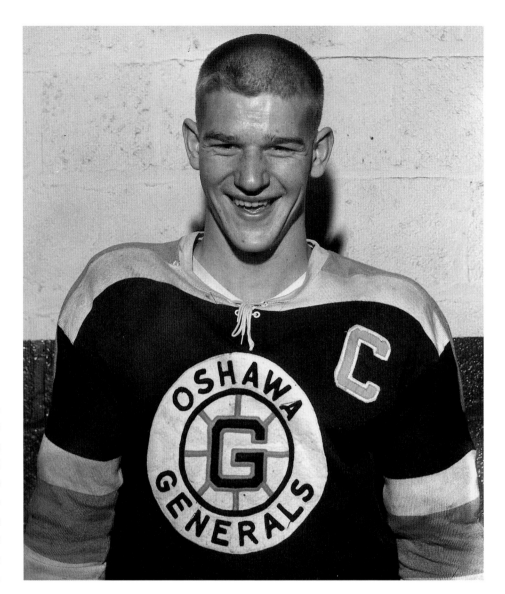

YOUNG BLOOD

As the captain of the Oshawa Generals, Bobby Orr averaged 33 goals a season—an astonishing total for a defenceman—and appeared on the cover of *Maclean's* magazine as a 17-year-old. Yet he was often homesick, and in the summers would hurry home to Parry Sound to work for the local butcher, in a clothing store, and as a bellhop.

meet with any lawyer, then dared to offer Orr $10,250 over two years. Eagleson contemptuously reminded him the New York Jets signed football rookie Joe Namath for *$400,000* over three years in 1965, and merrily pointed out that Orr didn't *have* to play for Boston right now—he could go to college. The threat worked, and in September 1966 Bobby Orr signed the largest rookie contract seen in the NHL—$80,000 over two years, including a $25,000 signing bonus.

In his first season, Orr won the Calder Trophy as rookie of the year, and in 1968, the first of his eight consecutive Norris Trophies as the NHL's best defenceman. Orr thrilled fans with his mercurial ice-long rushes, reinventing the game as he swirled and dashed, but people soon learned that he was not invincible.

His first knee operation came in August 1968, followed by another two months later. Even so, Orr's celestial talents pulled the Bruins upward, and his 1968 contract renewal sent NHL salaries in the same direction—with Eagleson's help. The lawyer's burgeoning reputation as a fearless liberator and expansion's demand for more players conspired to put Eagleson's hand into the biggest till he could imagine. Expansion had doubled the number of hockey jobs to 240, and Eagleson represented 180 of them.

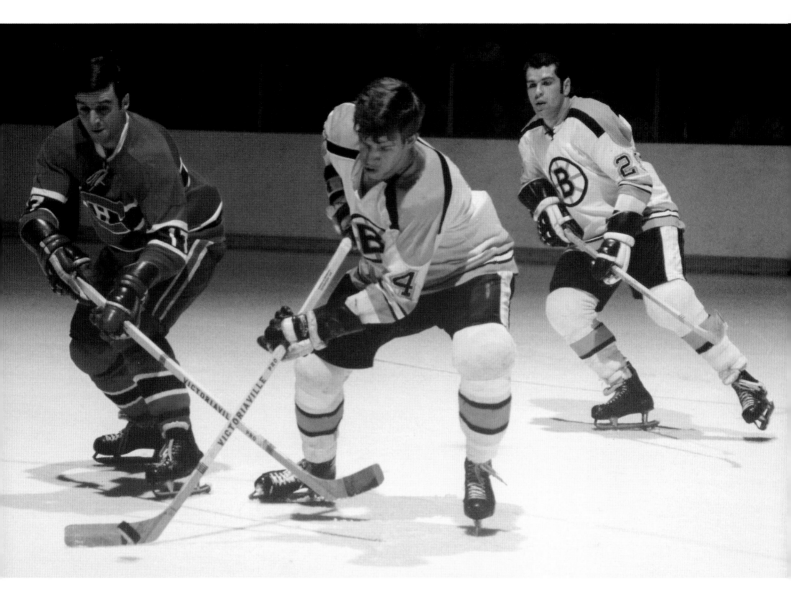

DUKE OF DEKE

(Above) Most players could only watch as Bobby Orr took the puck and worked his magic, reinventing the game with his speed, imagination and agility as he left opponents in his wake. The legendary Gordie Howe, when asked what he thought Orr's greatest move was, said, "Putting on his fucking skates." *(Left)* Alan Eagleson hugs Orr, his ticket to riches and power, after the 1976 Canada Cup, where despite his ravaged knees, Orr was Canada's best player. Having Bobby Orr as a client made Eagleson hockey's most powerful agent.

There was only one Bobby Orr, though, and teams scrambled to counter this defenceman who could create such imaginative offensive plays. The Bruins had mauled the competition in the 1970 playoffs and were poised to sweep the St. Louis Blues in the Stanley Cup finals. With steam rising off the Boston Garden ice in 90-degree humidity, the players wanted to end the sudden-death overtime fast, and Bobby Orr obliged. After blocking a clearing pass deep in the St. Louis zone, he slid the puck to Derek Sanderson.

When Sanderson whipped the puck onto Orr's stick and the star defenceman scored a heartbeat before a trip sent him flying through the air with his arms raised in triumph, "the Goal" became one of the most famous in Stanley Cup history. Orr's Cup winner was the culmination of a season in which he had rewritten the NHL record books, winning the Art Ross scoring title with 120 points; the Hart Trophy as league MVP; his third Norris Trophy; and the Conn Smythe Trophy as the most valuable postseason player—the first man to win all four trophies in the same year. And he was only 22 years old.

Yet Bobby Orr's ruined left knee prompted three more operations, and six years later, the Bruins didn't want him. A wounded Orr said, "If I were a horse, they'd probably shoot me." He signed with Chicago in 1976, had his sixth knee operation, sat out the entire 1978 season, and it was all over in 1979. At his press conference announcing his retirement, the 31-year-old Orr wept, still trying to separate his force of will from the force of pain. In the end, the player called the greatest ever by many sage hockey minds lost out to the ravages of the game that he graced with his genius.

LEAFS AND CANADIENS
BATTLE FOR THE
1967 STANLEY CUP

Canada celebrated its 100th birthday in 1967, and despite the nascent hostilities between French and English, the nation was in the mood for a party as Canadians dreamed about what their big rich country would accomplish in its next century. So, when the Toronto Maple Leafs and the Montreal Canadiens met in the 1967 Stanley Cup finals, it was a national birthday present for hockey's homeland: the boys in blue and white who were "Canada's Team" versus *les glorieux* in *bleu, blanc et rouge,* who were "Canada's Team," too, and religiously so in Quebec. A whiff of the Battle of the Plains of Abraham hung in the air, when the English General Wolfe defeated the French leader Montcalm in 1759, and the "two solitudes" meeting for the Centennial's Cup was a perfectly Canadian moment.

The teams had met four times previously for the big prize and had each won twice. Not much had been expected of the Maple Leafs in the 1967 Stanley Cup finals, and with Johnny Bower and Allan Stanley now over 40, and stalwarts "Red" Kelly, George Armstrong and Tim Horton on the wrong side of 35, sportswriters called the team "the Over the Hill Gang."

Terry Sawchuk and Johnny Bower shared the 1965 Vezina Trophy as the NHL's best goaltending duo, and in the 1967 Stanley Cup finals, they pooled 79 years of life experience between them. Newspapers called the 1967 Toronto Maple Leafs the "Over-the-Hill Gang" and the "Old Folks' Athletic Club," but Sawchuk and Bower laughed last, combining to beat Montreal in six games.

(Left) With the series tied at one game apiece, and the third game into its second overtime period tied at two, Bob Pulford flipped a Jim Pappin pass into the open net past Montreal's rookie goalie Rogatien Vachon to win the game for the Maple Leafs. Though Montreal would win Game 4, Toronto would take the series in six. *(Below, far left)* Thousands of Canadians crowd Parliament Hill in Ottawa on July, 1, 1967, to officially ring in the country's second century. Canadians coast-to-coast launched their own Centennial projects to contribute to the identity of the country that Marshall McLuhan famously said—that same year— was the only country that knew how to live without an identity. *(Below, near left)* Though the resplendent Pierre Elliott Trudeau was still Canada's justice minister, the Centennial celebrations launched the beginning of Trudeau-mania that would see him become prime minister the following year.

With Jean Beliveau, Henri Richard, Bobby Rousseau and Doug Harvey in their lineup, the Habs were a formidable bunch, but even so, they had finished only two points ahead of Toronto. After Montreal won the first game at home 6–2, it looked like a sweep of the "Leafs of Autumn" was in the works. Yet Johnny Bower—who had shared the Vezina Trophy with teammate Terry Sawchuk two seasons earlier—grew miserly, and Toronto won the second game 3–0. The third game in Toronto became a goalies' battle between the Habs' young Rogatien Vachon, who stopped 62 shots, and the ancient Bower, who stopped 54, before Bob Pulford won it for Toronto eight minutes into the second overtime period.

A cruel bolt of time struck down Bower in Game 4 when he injured his groin in the warm-up. Terry Sawchuk replaced him and had a bad game, giving the Canadiens a 6–2 win. A fan sent Sawchuk a telegram asking, "How much did you get?" and the tormented goalie, profoundly hurt, responded with the form that had made him a four-time Vezina winner. Toronto beat Montreal 4–1, and could now win it all at Maple Leaf Gardens.

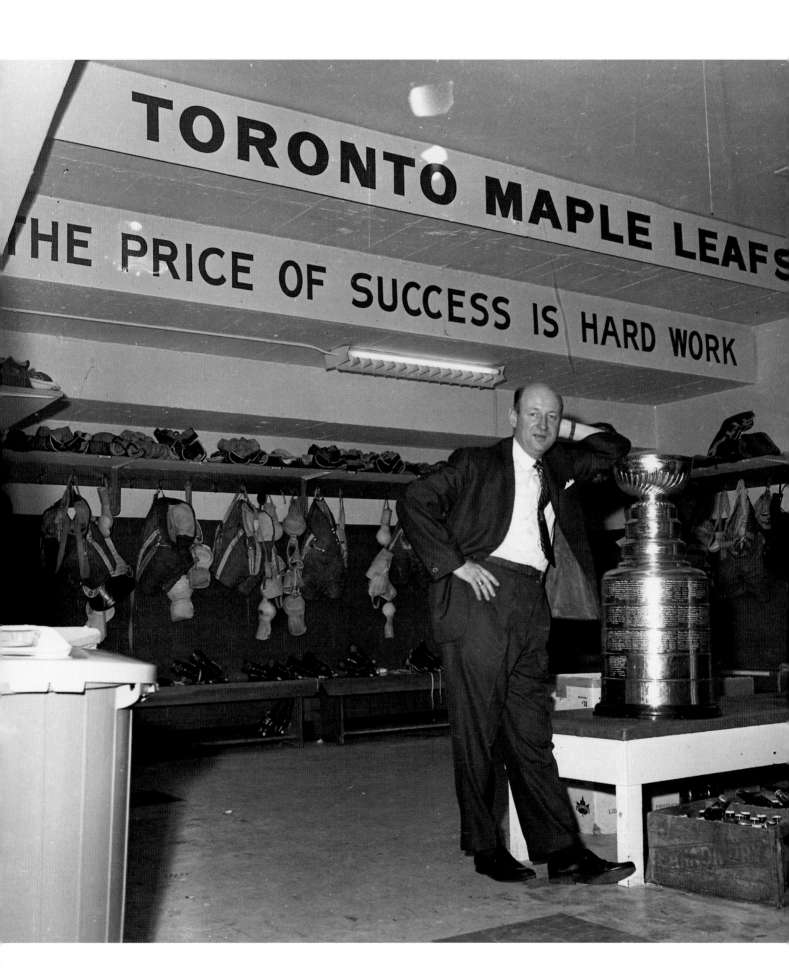

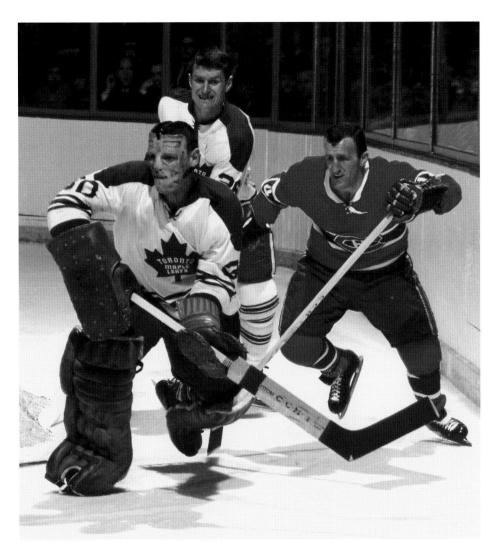

George Armstrong and Allan Stanley felt if the old boys could survive coach "Punch" Imlach's practices, they could take the Cup. For youngsters like Ron Ellis, the dressing room was electric when Imlach came in bearing a box of money. "This is what you're playing for," said Imlach, which was both true and a kick to their pride as players. They were playing to win.

And winning they were, up 2–1 with less than a minute left in the game. The Canadiens pulled Vachon and sent out an extra man for a face-off in the Toronto zone. Foster Hewitt, then in his 44th year of hockey broadcasting, called out that George Armstrong had scored into an empty net, and the Leafs had won their 11th Cup.

It was the end of the Leaf dynasty that had won four Cups in the 1960s, and also the last time that two of the "Original Six" teams would compete in the Stanley Cup finals. Though still possible for two Original Sixers to meet for the Cup, the vast NHL expansion in the intervening years has reduced the odds. And that expansion would begin the season following the Montreal–Toronto finals, with a whole new division of teams in Minnesota, Pittsburgh, Philadelphia, St. Louis, Los Angeles and Oakland to create a "truly North American" league—one without any new Canadian teams. As it had done in 1904, and 1924, the world's premier pro hockey league was heading south once more in search of a moneyed future. And the Leafs and the Canadiens had given the league a richly symbolic bon voyage.

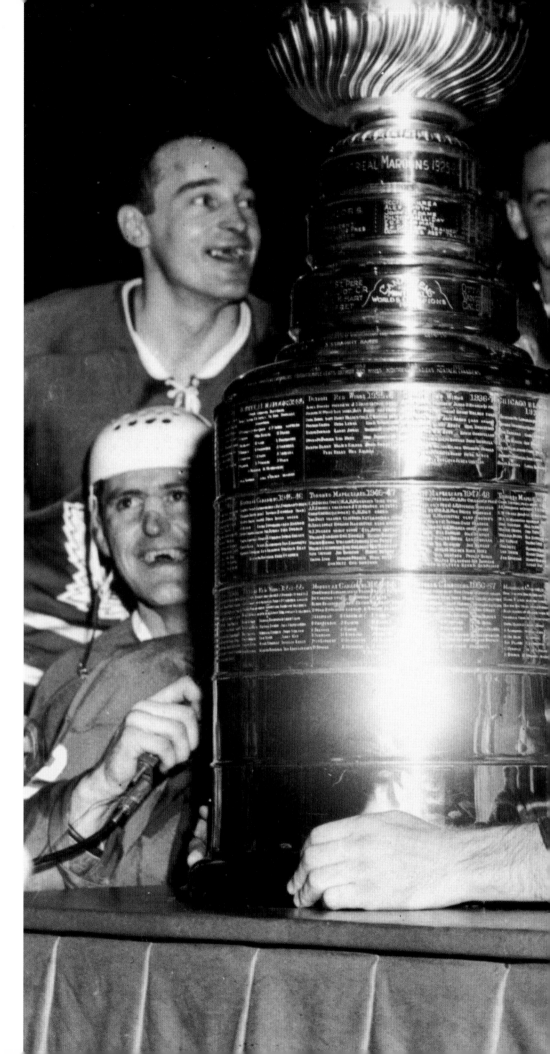

CUP TO REMEMBER
Captain George Armstrong embraces
the 1967 Stanley Cup surrounded
by the "Leafs of Autumn":
(from left to right) Allan Stanley, Frank
Mahovlich, unidentified man, Bob
Pulford, Bob Baun and "Red" Kelly.

THE TRAGEDY OF
TERRY SAWCHUK

Goaltenders are hockey's alchemists, with their spectacular saves spinning a leaden team's performance into gold, and just as easily turning team gold into lead with a muffed shot. The team's "last man" is a solo artist, and backstoppers tend to be contrary characters, bearing the weight of the team on their pads, and yet on a team by themselves, a contradiction of sometimes tragic solitude the ancient Greeks would have appreciated.

Terry Sawchuk was a team all by himself, posting a record 103 shutouts in his 20 seasons between the NHL pipes and winning four Vezina trophies as the best. Yet Sawchuk was also one of the most troubled men, and his death at 40 in May 1970 cast a cold epitaph not only on his unsurpassed career, but on the tragic goalies who came before him. The Montreal Canadiens' great netminder Georges Vezina, the man for whom the trophy is named, died in 1926 at age 39 of tuberculosis, and Chicago's Charlie Gardiner died of a brain hemorrhage while celebrating the Black Hawks' 1934 Stanley Cup victory. But Sawchuk topped them all.

Terry Sawchuk's goaltending style was like that of any great artist, a composite of the things he needed from the goalies who had gone before, then distilled—often quite literally—into something gloriously original. Diving, kicking, batting and teasing, Sawchuk considered a goal against him a personal insult, and posted 103 career shutouts in retort.

CROWD CONTROL

Terry Sawchuk discusses goaltending technique with the crowd at Maple Leaf Gardens. Sawchuk's relationship with fans was the same as with everyone else—often contrary. He usually played in pain thanks to his legion of injuries, and his dark psyche was a constant that led him right to the grave.

Those who saw Sawchuk put his body in front of speeding rubber thought him "the greatest," though he began hockey as the scoring champion of his Winnipeg Bantam A team. When the club's goalie quit, young Terry was put in net because his adored older brother, a goalie, had died at 17 of a heart murmur. Sawchuk's first game in goal wearing his dead brother's pads was such a good one that playing the position became a link with his brother.

Though he hoped to go to college, Sawchuk turned pro with the Omaha Knights when his father was laid up with a broken back. During a game in Houston, a stick caught him in the right eyeball, and instead of celebrating his 18th birthday, Sawchuk was in surgery. The doctor decided to cut out his eye, then changed his mind. Sawchuk went on to lead Omaha to the championship, won the rookie of the year award, and did so again the following season with Indianapolis, and again in the NHL, the first man to achieve this triple honour.

When Sawchuk made the big leagues, foreshadows of doom came early. In Sawchuk's second game for Detroit, Hall of Fame goalie George Hainsworth was killed in a car crash. Sawchuk would surpass Hainsworth's 94 NHL shutouts—becoming the first and only goalie to post 100, but the wins came at a price. Sawchuk took over 400 stitches in his face, and endured a herniated disk and severed wrist tendons. He suffered a broken right arm that didn't heal properly, and wound up shorter; a fractured instep; a punctured lung after a nearly fatal car accident; infectious mononucleosis; a ruptured appendix; and back surgery that lost him two inches in height.

As the years passed, "the Uke" became surly and withdrawn, a chain-smoker and hard drinker who preferred to be left alone. Sawchuk bounced around the league, from Detroit to Boston and back to Detroit, then on to Toronto. Despite his heroic play in the Leafs' 1967 Stanley Cup run, they let him go to the expansion Los Angeles Kings. In the kind of irony that dogged Sawchuk's career, the Leafs' directors voted the departing Sawchuk the greatest member of the team.

Sawchuk's last team was the New York Rangers, and on April 29, 1970, he returned to New York after an emotional visit to his estranged family, still worried about his father, who faced amputation of his legs after a car accident.

As Sawchuk entered the E & J Pub in Long Beach, New York, teammate Ron Stewart exited. An argument flared over the $190 Sawchuk owed for cleaning their rented house, and a fight ensued there, and again at home, where Sawchuk tripped over a metal barbecue grill. Sawchuk, who had played so many games in excruciating pain without a whimper, cried out in agony. After three major operations to remove blood from his lacerated liver, Terry Sawchuk died in hospital on June 1, 1970. A homicide investigation probed the truth of his last fight, but the autopsy report said the greatest goalie of all had been killed by a blood clot in his great, tormented heart.

DARK KNIGHT

(Below left) Terry Sawchuk is carried from his funeral mass by, among others, his New York Ranger manager-coach Emile Francis *(third on right)*, who had to identify Sawchuk at the morgue. *(Below)* Young Sawchuk beams as an Omaha Knight, but as the years passed, smiles were as rare as muffed shots for the tormented man called the best big-time goalie ever. Sawchuk's troubled soul often found liquid solace, and teammates knew that if he didn't say good morning, he wouldn't speak all day.

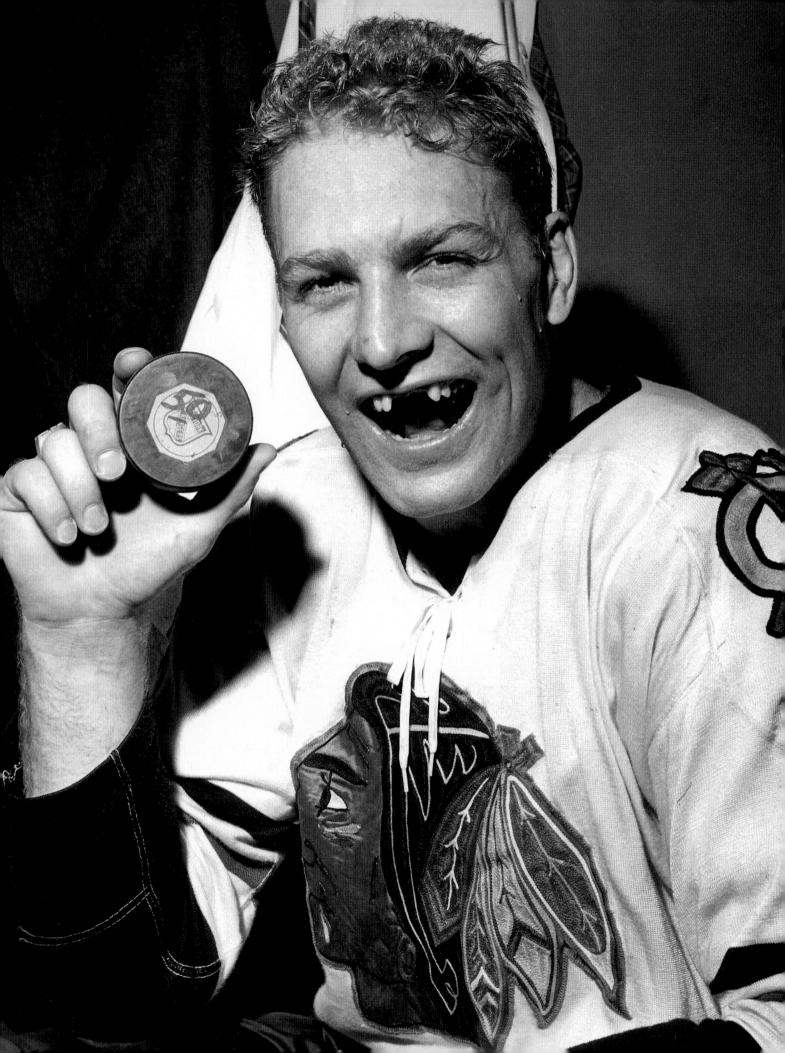

BOBBY HULL SIGNS WITH THE WHA

In the summer of 1972, two topics heated up the hockey world, and one of them was the World Hockey Association. Dreamed up by Californians Gary Davidson and Dennis Murphy, the WHA had been formed to give the NHL—after nearly 50 years as the only game in town—some competition. Ben Hatskin, owner of the WHA's Winnipeg Jets, lured 33-year-old Chicago Black Hawk Bobby Hull to the new league with a $2.75-million contract over 10 years, and the "Golden Jet" joined the WHA on June 27, 1972, accepting a cheque for $1 million as his advance.

Hull had come up from the St. Catharines juniors in 1957, and Chicago coach Rudy Pilous quickly teamed him up with big George Hay at centre and Murray Balfour at right wing to form the Million Dollar Line. Three years later Hull won the first of three Art Ross Trophies and was already touted as "the Golden Jet."

With forearms like Popeye's, Hull could put so much power into a shot that his backhand—once clocked at 96 miles per hour—was 10 miles per hour faster than an average player's forehand shot. In his 16 NHL seasons, he would score 610 goals,

Four of the first six 50-goal NHL seasons belong to Bobby Hull, but none compared to the toothless joy he showed upon notching his first in the Chicago Black Hawks' last regular-season game of the 1961–62 season.

become the first player to break the 50-goal mark (in 1966) held by "Rocket" Richard
and "Boom Boom" Geoffrion, and become the first NHL player to have six 50-goals-
or-more seasons.

When Hull became the first superstar to join the upstart WHA, luminaries and
journeymen alike jumped to new teams in Winnipeg, Houston, Los Angeles, Alberta,
Minnesota, Chicago, New York, Quebec, Ottawa, Philadelphia, Cleveland and New
England. In retaliation the NHL invoked the "reserve" clause, which had existed since
1917 and made NHL players the league's property for life

To prove its point further, the NHL forbade Bobby Hull and WHA players to do the
other thing that everyone was talking about in the summer of 1972—play hockey
against the Russians. The Canadian public mobilized in fury, for to shun Bobby Hull
because of his free enterprise was tantamount to treason. Canada's dashing prime
minister, Pierre Elliott Trudeau, sent a telegram reminding NHL president Clarence

Campbell "that Canada should be represented by its best hockey players, including Bobby Hull." Campbell haughtily told the prime minister he had been "misled," but the truth was that the NHL owners couldn't afford Hull. If he were forgiven his defection to the WHA, the NHL would effectively author the demise of its monopoly, and it wasn't going to do that.

Hull didn't play in the 1972 Canada–Soviet series, but he did play for seven seasons in the WHA before returning to the NHL in 1979 after the WHA folded and the Winnipeg Jets were assimilated by the old league. Though Hull was both rewarded and punished for exercising his right to work where he chose, his action amounted to an assault on pro hockey salaries, and forced the NHL to deal with the real power: the players and, increasingly, their agents. Never again would a cartel of owners be able to hold players hostage. In the new league's first season, when Hull won the WHA's most valuable player award, he won it for generations of pro hockey players.

PAUL HENDERSON
SCORES THE GOAL
OF A LIFETIME

Snow fell on Moscow on September 26, 1972, a harbinger that winter had come depressingly early as the Soviet Union's mighty team of hockey players entered the seventh of an eight-game series against a riotous crew of Canadians, whom they had tied once and were now leading three games to two. For Canada, the country that had given the world ice hockey and whose very essence was hanging on this series, 29-year-old Toronto Maple Leaf left winger Paul Henderson's hopes were those of a nation he was about to deliver.

Henderson was the archetypal hockey hero who had learned the game on frozen ponds, using Eaton's catalogues for shin pads, with his father—a Canadian National Railways worker—as coach. With linemates Ron Ellis (a fellow Leaf) and Bobby Clarke, Henderson's value lay in his hard work, which made him a hot-streak scorer. Henderson dreamed that the Canadians would emerge in triumph over the Red Machine, and he was going to make that dream come true. After all, he'd already scored the winning goal in Game 6, so why not again?

It is the most famous photograph in Canadian sports history, as defining as the moment when Paul Henderson scored the winner in Game 8 with 34 seconds left. Henderson is perhaps the only Canadian who doesn't have to account for what he thought at that moment. Later, he revealed he was thinking of his father, who had died four years earlier and would have loved that goal.

The Canadians' scouts had written off the Soviets as a bunch of amateurs, and their goalie, 20-year-old Vladislav Tretiak, as a Junior B sieve, but Canada lost the first game at the Montreal Forum 7–4, and national shock was the result. When the series moved to Vancouver on September 8, the shock had turned to derision, with the fans booing Team Canada in the warm-up. Once the Canadians were down 4–1 in a game they would lose 5–3, the booing and catcalls were merciless, and an angry Phil Esposito gave an emotional lecture on national television, telling Canadians that the team was trying its best, and if the Soviet fans booed *their* team, he would apologize.

Team Canada rallied on the road, freewheeling with their creativity and thuggish with their violence. And Paul Henderson was afloat on a sense that this was his time. With two minutes left in a 3–3 tie in Game 7, Henderson took a clearing pass from big

DAYS OF PASSION

(Above) Team Canada was vilified at home and abroad for its violent play. As Team Canada's on-ice padrone, Phil Esposito wore his heart as large on his sleeve as the stylized maple leaf on his torso. Here he receives a five-minute sentence for cutting Soviet defenceman Alexander Ragulin with a high stick. Despite his penalties, Esposito still found time to become the leading scorer in the Canada–Soviet Series, with seven goals and six assists. *(Right)* Ragulin was no angel himself, and was more than capable of a little bloody stickwork. *(Facing page)* Soviet militiamen set up a rinkside cordon during Game 8 to squash any affray that Canadian fans might start. Years later, former Soviet ambassador to Canada Alexander Yakolev would say the 1972 series was the beginning of *glasnost* and *perestroika*.

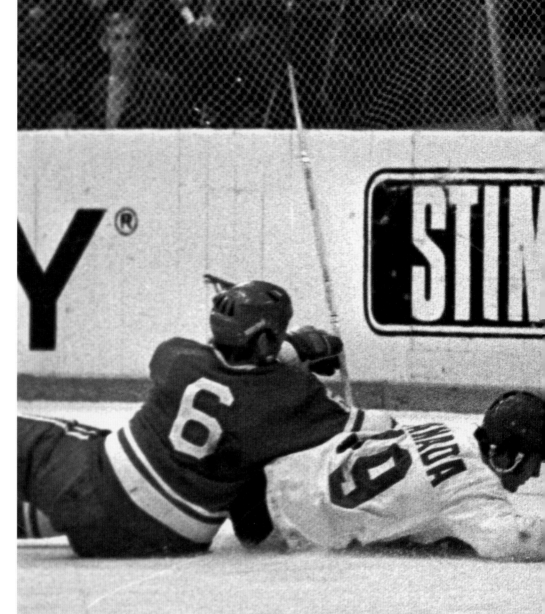

As Peter Mahovlich raises his arms
in triumph at the end of Game 8,
Soviet defenceman Viktor Kuzkin
raises a hand in military salute. After
the bloody conflict of these 27
days in September 1972, the end
feels more like war than hockey.

Serge Savard near his own blue line, swung around the Russian defence, and picked a little spot of paradise just above Tretiak's right elbow. The Canadians in the stands went wild, as if the team had won the whole prize. With the series tied at three wins apiece and one tie, Canada could win it all. But so could the Soviets.

With one period left in an emotional, feisty Game 8, the Canadians were down 5–3 and desperate. Esposito started the climb to glory at 2:27 of the third period, whacking in his own rebound. Ten minutes later he shook off two Soviet players to let loose a blast at Tretiak. The rebound popped out to Yvan "the Roadrunner" Cournoyer, and with seven minutes left, the game was tied.

The Canadians caught the scent of bloody victory. In the third period alone, Team Canada outshot the Soviets 13–5, and now Henderson knew he could complete his mission, but Phil Esposito's line wouldn't come off the ice. After calling out three times, Henderson lured Pete Mahovlich off and jumped over the boards. Cournoyer

fired a pass behind Henderson, and Esposito beat three Soviet players to it, then fired
it at Tretiak. The rebound came back to Henderson, alone now in front of Tretiak. He
shot the puck, and Tretiak made a pad save going down. The puck came back to Henderson, he shot again, and scored. Canada had won back its birthright.

Paul Henderson became a national icon, immortalized in posters, coins, stamps
and in memory with his arms upraised after the winning puck went in, summoning
the joy of the cosmos. People packed Montreal's Dorval Airport to greet the team;
they lined up in the rain in Toronto's Nathan Phillips Square to see their heroes. Phil
Esposito kept the emotional promise he made in Vancouver to apologize to the country. "You people have proved me wrong," he told the crowd. "You've proved the rest
of us wrong." And every Canadian over the age of four would forever remember
where they were on that day, at that moment, when Paul Henderson won back the
game of hockey.

MAN OF DESTINY

Like a man possessed, Paul
Henderson puts the puck behind
Vladislav Tretiak despite being
tackled from behind. The goal won
Game 7 for Canada 4–3, and set the
stage for the completion of
Henderson's mythic exploits.

AN ALL-AMERICAN
MIRACLE ON ICE

In February 1980 the United States was in an anxious mood. The Iran Hostage Crisis was in its third month, and despite the escape of six U.S. embassy aides with Canadian help, the Islamic militants of Ayatollah Khomeini showed no inclination to release their 52 American prisoners any time soon. The nuclear doomsday clock inched closer to midnight, too, despite the fact that U.S. president Jimmy Carter and his Soviet counterpart, Leonid Brezhnez, had signed Strategic Arms Limitation Treaty II the previous June. The Soviets were embroiled in a hot war in Afghanistan and still in the deep freeze of their three-decade Cold War with the United States, and though Ronald Reagan had not yet called them an "evil empire," that's how the Americans viewed them when the U.S. men's hockey team met the mighty Soviets for a shot at an Olympic gold medal at Lake Placid, New York.

The United States hadn't won an Olympic gold at hockey since the 1960 "Miracle on Ice" at Squaw Valley, California, when a crew of American long shots knocked off the world's hockey powers from Canada, Sweden and the Soviet Union before unequivocally beating the Czechs 9–4 to win the gold medal. The effect on hockey had

In a tableau reminiscent of the statue of U.S. Marines raising Old Glory at Iwo Jima, Team U.S.A. celebrates its improbable Olympic victory in 1980. Playing in front of a euphoric hometown crowd, the Americans beat Finland 4–2 to win the gold medal. "Do you believe in miracles?" asked ABC announcer Al Michaels. The answer was on the ice.

been something like the effect on the birth rate nine months after a winter power outage, with a surge in young Americans clamouring to imitate their golden heroes on ice.

Twenty years later, though, the U.S. Olympic hockey team was no further ahead than their Squaw Valley ancestors, and pundits felt the team was outmatched. But the American Olympic hopefuls thought otherwise. Buoyant from their tie with the vigorous and canny Swedes in the first game, they went on to beat the Czechs, Norwegians, Romanians and West Germans to come face-to-face with the reigning world champs—the Soviets.

The Soviet Union had walloped the Americans 11–3 in an exhibition game a few days earlier, and were the model of icy discipline and merciless skill, playing with such scientific precision that jealous cries of "robots" and "machines" were regularly hurled at them. The Americans, on the other hand, were a cliché too naked for even the most desperate Hollywood hack: an excited, emotional crew of college boys, coached by the University of Minnesota's Herb Brooks, who dressed in loud plaid jackets as if auditioning for a car-lot job just in case the hockey gig didn't work out. If that wasn't enough, defenceman Dave Christian's father and uncle had been on the 1960 gold-medal team, a fact that promised the United States its very own family storybook ending if it could only do the impossible.

THE FIRST MIRACLE

(Facing page) Lowly Team U.S.A.'s players showed early in the 1960 Winter Olympics in Squaw Valley, California, that they might be giants. Here, in the opening round, the Americans came from behind to beat the mighty Czechs 7–5. Just over a week later, the Americans came from behind again to beat the Czechs 9–4 to win the country's first hockey gold medal. *(Above)* The underdog U.S. hockey team celebrates its victory over the Soviets. With the game tied at two, the Russians pounded relentlessly, but Billy Christian's late third-period goal was good enough to put the U.S. team into the final against Czechoslovakia.

THE SECOND MIRACLE

(Above) Team U.S.A. coach Herb Brooks discusses strategy with players at Lake Placid. The 1980 U.S. team was rich with links to the past, including Coach Brooks, who had been the last player cut from the 1960 squad. *(Facing page)* Team U.S.A. goalie James Craig finds the puck in the 1980 Olympic gold-medal round. Like Jack McCartan in 1960, Craig was the Americans' last hope, allowing only 15 goals in seven games, and holding off the enemy three times so the United States could come from behind to win.

The collision of these two wildly different teams generated a game of transcendent passion, with the crowd-fuelled Americans wearing hate on their red, white and blue sleeves for everything the Communist Soviets signified in 1980. Led by goalie Jim Craig, Neal Broten, Rob McLanahan and Ken Morrow, all of whom would rise to the NHL, the write-off Americans pulled off another Miracle on Ice with a last-minute goal to give them a 4–3 win over the Soviets, leading to a three-goal third-period comeback against Finland to win the gold.

The glorious victory not only shot throughout a nation craving a triumphant underdog, but resonated right through to the shocking moment in September 1996 when the United States beat Canada to win hockey's first World Cup. In a country in which hockey had long been played but had never been a passion, the 1980 Miracle on Ice fired up the hearts of a generation, giving the United States the will to produce hockey players who could beat the world. John Leclair, a star forward on the United States' 1996 World Cup team, said that the 1980 triumph had changed the nation. "Every kid in the United States wanted to play for the Olympic team after that game."

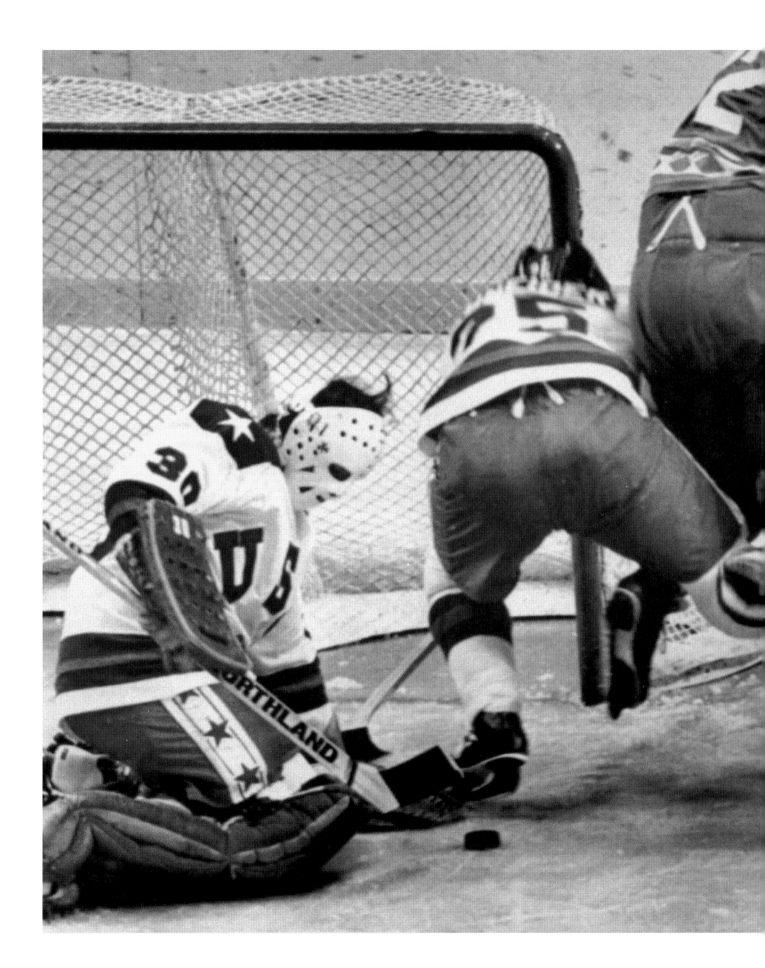

24

EDMONTON DEALS
WAYNE GRETZKY
TO LOS ANGELES

In May 1988 he had raised his fourth Stanley Cup above his head to a jubilant kingdom of thousands in his city of Edmonton. In July he had married the blonde American actress Janet Jones in a lavish ceremony complete with a red-coated honour guard in Edmonton's St. Joseph's Cathedral Basilica. Less than a month after hockey's royal wedding, as the majesty and his bride were making plans for their glorious future, he was dispatched on August 9, 1988, to the Los Angeles Kings, a team at least more nominally suited to his stature. It was a trade that shocked Canada, for to trade the sport's greatest player meant that Wayne Gretzky was not at the centre of the universe, but just another body in motion around the sun.

Now, indisputably, the sport that fuelled the winter dreams of the world's cold countries was stoked by cold hard cash. But that fact had already been apparent when Wayne Gretzky was bought and sold as a teenager and the rival leagues of the WHA and NHL had laboured hard to destroy each other with money. Yet after 10 seasons in Edmonton, the 27-year-old centre had modest thoughts of setting up house in Edmonton with his new bride, raising a family, and growing old.

After being swept in four games by the New York Islanders in the 1983 Stanley Cup finals, the young Edmonton Oilers—who were so in awe of where they were, they used to sing "Let's Go Oilers" on the bench—turned the tables in 1984 and ended the Islanders' four-Cup dynasty. Wayne Gretzky called his first hoisting of Lord Stanley's trophy his "sweetest moment in hockey."

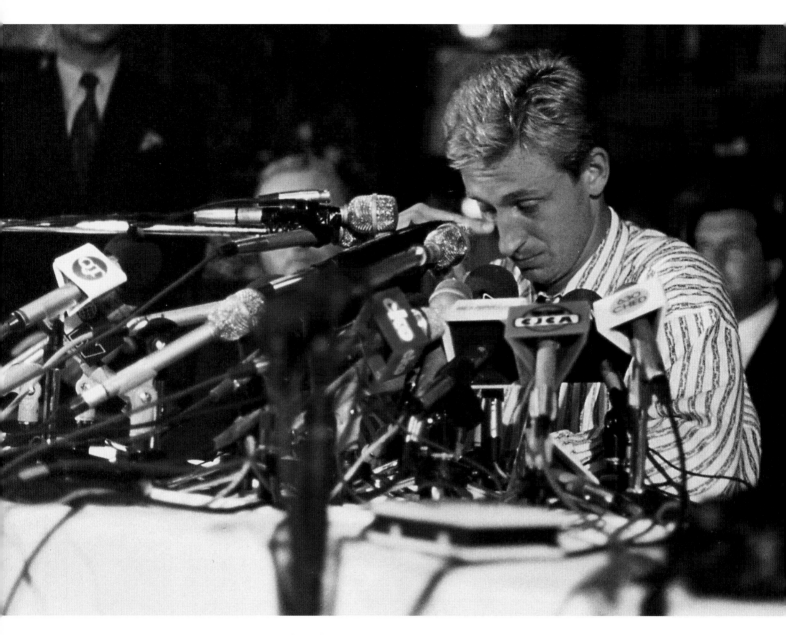

There had been whisperings in the hockey world for a few months before the trade that Edmonton owner Peter Pocklington was shopping Gretzky, upset that "the Great One" wouldn't sign the kind of contract the cash-strapped Pocklington needed to put the Oilers on the stock market and keep them his. Nelson Skalbania, a Vancouver tycoon who had originally signed the 17-year-old Gretzky to the Indianapolis Pacers of the WHA, convinced the Winnipeg Jets to take Gretzky's expensive package.

Enter Bruce McNall, a portly and fast-talking concoction that could only come out of Hollywood. McNall, who had made his fortune dealing in ancient coins, had branched out to mogul pastimes such as racehorses, movies, and now, the Los Angeles Kings. He knew that Gretzky was just the kind of glittering jewel he needed to fill all those empty seats in Los Angeles.

Six days after his wedding, Gretzky received a phone call from McNall saying he had permission from Edmonton to do the unthinkable. After recovering his emotional balance, Gretzky went into cold-eyed negotiation for his departure, and when it was all over, he and his protector Marty McSorley, along with Mike Krushelnyski, went to Los Angeles in exchange for the Kings' great white hope Jimmy Carson, Martin Gelinas, three first-round draft picks, and $15 million in Canadian funds.

Gretzky wept at his press conference, and the shock waves thundered across the nation. Elected officials stood up in provincial legislatures and the House of Parliament in Ottawa and decried Pocklington's whoring of a national treasure, while Edmonton's mayor compared the loss of Gretzky to the desecration of the city's beautiful river valley. Canadians couldn't find it in their hearts to blame Wayne, and so they aimed their wrath at his pregnant wife, smearing her as the Yoko Ono of the Oilers who wrecked a dynasty so that she could advance her "starlet" career in Hollywood.

Despite bitter predictions that Gretzky would shrivel in the L.A. sun, "the Great One" scored on his first shot in his first game as a King. Gretzky's dazzling star power made hockey the hottest ticket in Los Angeles, and soon there were NHL teams in San Jose, Anaheim, Tampa Bay, and Miami, for his drawing power brought pro hockey to Sun Belt, U.S.A.

The man himself went on to win another Hart Trophy in his first season as the Kings bounced the Edmonton Oilers in the first round of the Stanley Cup playoffs. In his second and third seasons as a King, Gretzky won the Art Ross Trophy as the NHL's leading point scorer, but in his seven years with Los Angeles he could never accomplish the one thing he wanted most—another Stanley Cup.

CALIFORNIA KING

(Below left) Los Angeles King Wayne Gretzky becomes the new scoring champion of the NHL on October 15, 1989, appropriately enough, in Edmonton. Gretzky broke his idol Gordie Howe's seemingly insurmountable NHL record of 1,850 points. (Below) Gretzky returned to Edmonton's Coliseum on October 20, 1988. Proving that bygones were just that, he scored on his first shift.

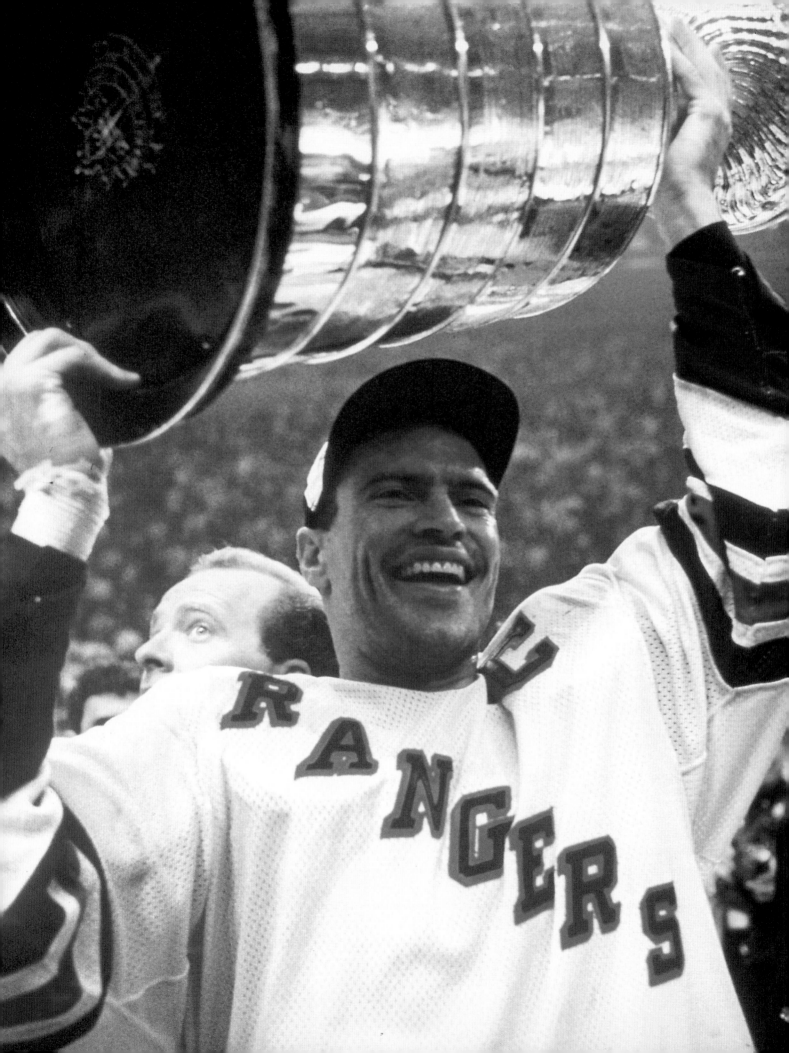

THE RANGERS
END THE CURSE

The last time the New York Rangers had drunk from the world's most distinguished champagne jug came in the spring of 1940, when the Broadway Blueshirts dispatched the Toronto Maple Leafs in six games to take their third Stanley Cup since their birth in 1926. Their victory, however, was desecrated by an act so profane that it seemed to many in the hockey world that the Rangers would never escape "the Curse" with which the hockey gods had zapped them.

The Stanley Cup—or Holy Grail to true believers—had suffered indignities before, having served as a flower pot, been left by the roadside by a champagne-chilled crew of Montreal Canadiens, booted into the frozen Rideau Canal by the drunken Ottawa Silver Seven and, in its hitherto most shameful abuse, used as a toilet by Detroit Red Wing Gordon Pettinger during a drunken Stanley Cup victory celebration in 1937.

Among professional hockey players who have and haven't won the Cup, there is a mystical feeling that you mess with it at your peril, and those with the effrontery even to hug it or kiss it before they've won it shouldn't expect to win it ever. So when

From the depth of joy on his face, it's easy to forget this is Captain Mark Messier's sixth Stanley Cup as he becomes the first Ranger captain to hoist the Cup at home. In exchange for helping to finance Madison Square Garden, John Ringling made a deal giving his circus tenancy every April. Thus exiled by the circus, the Rangers won their previous Cups on the road.

Ranger president Colonel John Reed Kilpatrick decided to celebrate Madison Square Garden's fully paid-up mortgage by burning the deed in the bowl of the Stanley Cup, his sacrifice to Mammon had defiled not only the chalice, but the entire temple. And the Rangers would suffer.

For the next 54 years, the team watched its championship hopes melt with the winter ice, managing to make it to the finals just twice, and losing both times. After finishing in last place in the Patrick Division in 1993, the Rangers roared back in 1994, topping the league with 112 points and the widespread prediction that with the fearless might of captain Mark Messier and the hockey gifts of Brian Leetch and Mike Richter, this year "the Curse" would be slain.

But "the Curse" fought back. With the Rangers up three games to one over the Vancouver Canucks, New Yorkers were planning the victory parade with their team leading 3–1 at the end of the first period. But when the Stanley Cup was brought up from Madison Square Garden's basement to the concourse level in preparation for its inevitable presentation, an extraordinary thing happened: the Canucks went on an unanswered five-goal run.

Then, in what some have called the greatest hockey game ever played at the Pacific Coliseum, the Canucks tied the series with a 4–1 win. There had only been 10 seventh games in the Stanley Cup finals since 1939, and now there was going to be another one.

In the final game, the Rangers were leading 3–2 when Vancouver's Nathan Lafayette found a Geoff Courtnall pass on his stick. With a powerful stroke, he one-timed the puck and sent it rocketing past Ranger goalie Mike Richter. For a moment, New Yorkers held their collective breath, but the post sent the puck ricocheting back out in a ping that knelled the passing of "the Curse" for their beloved team. And once again, on June 14, 1994, the 102-year-old Cup lit up Broadway the way it had last done as a whippersnapper of 48.

RANGERS UNHEXED

(Below) In only their second playoffs (1928), the New York Rangers won their first Stanley Cup—the last time the trophy was won so quickly by an "expansion" team. GM and coach Lester Patrick *(standing, centre)*, then 44, poses in uniform, a right earned when he heroically donned the goalie pads to substitute for injured Lorne Chabot in Game 2. *(Facing page)* When the buzzer sounds to end Game 7 of the 1994 Stanley Cup finals, Madison Square Garden breaks into jubilation as the Rangers win their first Cup in 54 years, and "the Curse" vanishes through the roof.

AFTERWORD

A few years ago a television commercial for after-shave featured Don Cherry, hockey's defender of the faith (in his case, a sacred Canadian creed besieged by cunning foreign devils), waking up to a radio announcer screaming, "The Russians have won the Stanley Cup!" Shocked to the cuffs of his maple-leafed skivvies at such heresy, Cherry wallops himself in the face with a bracing dose of the product being hawked, and so revived, escapes his worst nightmare ever.

Well, the Russians *have* won the Stanley Cup—not yet as a nation, but as one crucial fifth of the champion Detroit Red Wings for two years' running. America's men have won the World Cup, while American women took the first women's Olympic hockey gold at Nagano—the same venue where the Czechs took revenge for the brutal Soviet invasion of their country in 1968 by beating the Russians to win the men's gold.

Hockey's future looks just as polyglot, for in the 1998 world junior championships, Finland beat Russia for the most glittering prize, while the kids from Switzerland won their first medal ever, a bronze, after taking the Czechs 4–3 in a shoot-out. Glorious Canada—expected, as always, to win—received a 6–3 humiliation from mighty Kazakhstan, a squad so destitute they had to scrounge hockey sticks from other teams to make it through the tournament.

Though they had come into the 1998 Winter Olympics as a long shot with fewer NHL players than favoured Canada, United States, Sweden, Russia and Finland, the Czech Republic's indomitable goalie Dominik Hasek proudly displays his country's first gold medal in 17 Olympic tournaments. Given the galloping internationalization of the game, the future of Olympic hockey promises to be as gloriously varied as its players.

Meanwhile, the Canadian media spat and hissed at the hubris and treason of it all: here was Canada, which so graciously gave the world this beautiful sport, now being hosed by a bunch of ungrateful interlopers on any arena, anywhere. If this kind of complacency continued, Canada would soon be ranked somewhere near China or Mexico as a world hockey power.

Back in the NHL, things weren't much better. The Magnificent Mario Lemieux—who triumphed over Hodgkin's disease and an aggravating back injury—refused to return for another magnificent season, citing the clutch-and-grab tedium on ice as too soul-destroying to make it worth his while. Still, there was Eric Lindros to take his place, hailed for years now as hockey's next great lion. Yet Lindros seemed increasingly like a white—and orange-and-black—elephant, full of sound and fury as he thundered about the ice, but unable to lead Canada to an Olympic medal, or Philadelphia past the first round of the playoffs. And while Lindros faltered, Paul Kariya, the artist who plays for hockey's cartoon, the Mighty Ducks, was knocked flat by such a vicious cross-check that his subsequent concussion has cast doubt on whether his genius is lost to him—and to hockey—forever.

And he wasn't the only player sidelined by a debilitating head injury, though his retired brethren laid to rest a major headache when Alan Eagleson was finally sent to jail for defrauding the men whose blood and sweat had made him rich and powerful. It seemed to some that with the fall of Eagleson—and some players have argued he didn't fall far or hard enough—and in Canada's international embarrassments that hockey had lost both its virtue and its birth certificate, and now tottered along with cynical millennial angst, trailing blue and orange comet tails signifying nothing except commerce.

Still, the globalization of hockey's Olympus simply means that the next generation of defining moments will come from a landscape whose deeds of glory and perfidy will often be performed by people bearing passports that aren't written in English or French. Hockey will gain shape and colour from these cosmopolitan changes, much as it did when it moved from frozen ponds into covered rinks, when players stopped using branches for sticks and horse manure for pucks as equipment and rules were perfected and tribal loyalties were defined, and when the game's combatants became professional and mobile and were able to sell their superiority for cold hard cash to the highest bidder to continue their quest to be the best in the world.

Even so, the pinnacle had always been the goal, and the sport's energy came from the fuel of those competing to be champions. This goal hasn't changed, but the competitors have, and their chapters will build on the ones that came before to add a richness that those aboriginals, Europeans and North Americans who wrote the sport's early chapters would appreciate.

For some, change equals chaos, but it won't stop hockey's next generation of defining moments, when we might see a women's pro league with a trophy to rival Lord Stanley's, or a kid from Helsinki or Prague rewrite the seemingly untouchable Book of Wayne Gretzky. As the game migrates to unknown frontiers, perhaps some future World Cup of Hockey will be as popular as that of soccer, and every day during the tournament two billion people will pause in worship of the world's other "most beautiful game." Who knows? Perhaps China or Mexico will capture hockey's World Cup in 2098, while my own abashed crew of heartbreakers called the Vancouver Canucks will, with luck or providence, win their first Stanley Cup sometime before that.

It was in Vancouver on a warm spring night during the 1998 Stanley Cup playoffs that I caught a glimpse of hockey's future, one which looked remarkably like its past. When I stepped out to replenish the household libations in between periods of a critical game, I was caught by the clacking of wood and metal coming from kids playing roller hockey on the asphalt of the school down the street—as I myself had done in this city 25 years earlier, if not quite in June. Though the kids could have been watching the game on TV, they chose instead to play it, and create their own glories. As ever, hockey has its definition in the hearts of young players around the world. And unless human nature changes unfathomably between now and then, a few of these unknowns will one day create their own perfect moments to let the world know what they mean to hockey.